PlanNC Guidebook
A Practitioner's Guide to Preparing Streamlined Community Plans

Ben Hitchings, FAICP, CZO
with Jim Joyce and Adam Lovelady
August 2021

UNC | SCHOOL OF GOVERNMENT

The School of Government at the University of North Carolina at Chapel Hill works to improve the lives of North Carolinians by engaging in practical scholarship that helps public officials and citizens understand and improve state and local government. Established in 1931 as the Institute of Government, the School provides educational, advisory, and research services for state and local governments. The School of Government is also home to a nationally ranked Master of Public Administration program, the North Carolina Judicial College, and specialized centers focused on community and economic development, information technology, and environmental finance.

As the largest university-based local government training, advisory, and research organization in the United States, the School of Government offers up to 200 courses, webinars, and specialized conferences for more than 12,000 public officials each year. In addition, faculty members annually publish approximately 50 books, manuals, reports, articles, bulletins, and other print and online content related to state and local government. The School also produces the *Daily Bulletin Online* each day the General Assembly is in session, reporting on activities for members of the legislature and others who need to follow the course of legislation.

Operating support for the School of Government's programs and activities comes from many sources, including state appropriations, local government membership dues, private contributions, publication sales, course fees, and service contracts.

Visit sog.unc.edu or call 919.966.5381 for more information on the School's courses, publications, programs, and services.

Michael R. Smith, DEAN
Aimee N. Wall, SENIOR ASSOCIATE DEAN
Jennifer Willis, ASSOCIATE DEAN FOR DEVELOPMENT

FACULTY

Whitney Afonso	Norma Houston (on leave)	David W. Owens
Trey Allen (on leave)	Cheryl Daniels Howell	Obed Pasha
Gregory S. Allison	Willow S. Jacobson	William C. Rivenbark
Lydian Altman	James L. Joyce	Dale J. Roenigk
David N. Ammons	Robert P. Joyce	John Rubin
Maureen Berner	Diane M. Juffras	Jessica Smith
Frayda S. Bluestein	Dona G. Lewandowski	Meredith Smith
Kirk Boone	Adam Lovelady	Carl W. Stenberg III
Mark F. Botts	James M. Markham	John B. Stephens
Anita R. Brown-Graham	Christopher B. McLaughlin	Charles Szypszak
Peg Carlson	Kara A. Millonzi	Thomas H. Thornburg
Connor Crews	Jill D. Moore	Shannon H. Tufts
Leisha DeHart-Davis	Jonathan Q. Morgan	Emily Turner
Shea Riggsbee Denning	Ricardo S. Morse	Jeffrey B. Welty (on leave)
Sara DePasquale	C. Tyler Mulligan	Richard B. Whisnant
Jacquelyn Greene	Kimberly L. Nelson	Brittany L. Williams
Margaret F. Henderson	Kristi A. Nickodem	Teshanee T. Williams

25 24 23 22 21   1 2 3 4 5
ISBN 978-1-64238-040-8

Cover image credits (clockwise from top) Town of Benson, Town of Apex, and Ben Hitchings.

Contents

Acknowledgments vii

Introduction... 1

Step 1: Summarize Existing Conditions 9

Step 2: Engage the Community 13

Step 3: Set Goals and Policies 21

Step 4: Map the Future 25

Step 5: Select Implementation Strategies 31

Step 6: Draft and Adopt the Plan............................. 35

Step 7: Move to Action 39

Conclusion 43

Worksheets and Templates 45

   Template 1A. Sample Project Timeline........................46

   Template 1B. Existing Conditions Data Worksheet 47

   Template 2A. Community Engagement Plan 59

   Template 2B. Sample Interview Questions for
     Town Staff...63

   Template 2C. Interview Questions for
     Key Stakeholders...64

   Template 2D. Sample Community Workshop Agenda 65

Template 2E. Governing Board Progress Report 67

Template 3A. Public Engagement
   Synthesis Worksheet...69

Template 3B. Developing Goals Worksheet 72

Template 4A. Mapping Checklist: Creating a
   Future Land Use Map 75

Template 5A. Implementation Toolbox 77

Template 5B. Sample Implementation Checklist........79

Template 6A. Plan Outline 80

Template 6B. Public Hearing Cheat Sheet...................81

Template 7A. Sample Project Charter 83

Acknowledgments

Special thanks go to the UNC-Chapel Hill Department of City and Regional Planning 2021 Spring Workshop class for conducting research on data sources and public engagement techniques, and for preparing Templates 1B on Existing Conditions Data and 2A on Community Engagement Plans. The class included masters students Austin Amandolia, Qing Cheng, Katie Koffman, Cheng Ma, Amy Sechrist, Shane Sweeney, Lauren Turner, Ellery Walker, Carly Wang, and Maggie Wiener, and was taught by Lecturer John Tallmadge.

Photos courtesy of the Town of Knightdale.

Introduction

In the early 2000s, community leaders in Knightdale, North Carolina, looked down First Avenue and saw an opportunity to rebuild the town's main street. A fire in the 1940s destroyed much of the traditional downtown, and suburban expansion in the late 20th century directed public and private investment elsewhere. But the community had a vision to reestablish a vibrant downtown. An ongoing planning effort, including a comprehensive plan and downtown plan, helped the town secure $20 million in public improvements in downtown. The resulting walkable main street and community park have catalyzed more than $250 million in private investment to date and enabled the town to create a vibrant new central gathering place for the community.

Across North Carolina, communities like Knightdale are using the power of planning to improve their communities in ways large and small. But often, the hardest part is getting started. This guidebook describes how to prepare an impactful and streamlined plan for the future. In so doing, communities can develop a shared vision that energizes local stakeholders and catalyzes lasting community improvements.

Communities and leaders face challenging questions. Questions of prosperity and opportunity, character and preservation, resilience and revitalization. Questions at the heart of local land use planning. How can we revitalize downtown? How do we protect our agricultural lands and property? What investments should we make to lure new economic development? What steps should we take to ensure good housing options? How do we make sure residents are safe during the next weather emergency? What aspects of our community do we want to preserve and what aspects do we want to change? Community planning seeks answers to critical questions.

Guiding Principles for PlanNC Guidebook

In order to accomplish an effective—yet streamlined—planning process, this guidebook and the process it outlines are built on the following guiding principles:

- focused on land use planning,

- grounded in key data for current conditions and trends,

- guided by authentic community input,

- informed by planning best practices, and

- aligned with practical implementation strategies.

A good land use plan is a community's own vision for the future. A good plan is a roadmap for finding that future. And a good plan reflects the current conditions of a place as well as the actions for moving forward. To accomplish such lofty goals, a good plan must be authentic to the place, built on substance, and framed for action. This guidebook strives to help communities across the state craft plans that are authentic to the particular community, that are founded on accurate data and analysis, and that chart a clear path forward so the community can be a truly great place for all who live, work, and visit.

The re-birth of downtown Knightdale followed that path of careful planning and strong implementation. In 2003 the community crafted and adopted a comprehensive plan. Additional planning efforts followed: a downtown plan (2007), a pedestrian plan (2013), and an updated comprehensive plan (2018). The community vision forged through these efforts helped the town pass a bond referendum and secure grants to invest more than $20 million in public improvements. The sidewalk and streetscape improvements have set the stage for a vibrant First Avenue. The new Knightdale Station Park, including a veterans memorial, amphitheater, splashpad, and more, is a gathering place for the community. New businesses and restaurants have opened, new homes have been built, and the vision for a revitalized downtown is coming to fruition.

In addition to the on-the-ground success, Knightdale's efforts have garnered praise. In 2019 the *KnightdaleNext 2035 Comprehensive Plan* won the statewide award for small community comprehensive plan, and in 2020 First Avenue was recognized as one of North Carolina's Great Places by the state chapter of the American Planning Association.

Who Can Use This Guidebook?

The guidebook is designed for communities and planning professionals wishing to quickly develop a meaningful comprehensive plan or land use plan using limited resources—especially for communities with limited capacity for land use planning. The publication also contains many ideas and suggestions that would be helpful for anyone preparing a community plan.

There are many scales and dimensions of planning. The needs of a large city are different from the needs of a small town. Communities experiencing fast growth rates face different issues than communities with stable or declining population. Moreover, when it comes to community land use planning, there are many methods to utilize, many topics to address, and many factors to consider. In addition, communities approach planning with different resources and different expectations. Some local governments have already adopted comprehensive plans or land use plans and are actively maintaining these documents. Other communities have not yet adopted plans but have the capacity and expertise required to conduct the necessary drafting and updates, or the resources needed to hire consultants

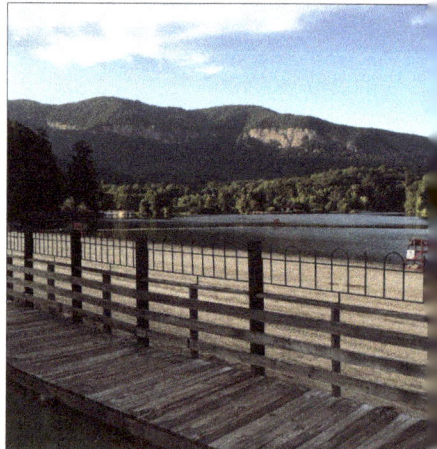

Photos by Ben Hitchings.

or other service providers to assist them in doing so. As a result, we encourage guidebook users to customize their planning approach based on their particular community circumstances. A number of local governments lack planning capacity, expertise, and/or resources and thus need help in meeting drafting and updating requirements. This guidebook is intended especially as a resource for these communities and for the service providers who assist them.

Why Plan?

"Planning" is a broad term that encompasses many different concepts. This guidebook is focused on local land use and comprehensive planning, especially in small towns. As discussed more below, there are certain state law requirements for local land use planning, but also there are valuable underlying reasons for good community planning. That process of local planning allows communities to consider and answer critical questions like, "How do we encourage opportunity and prosperity?" "What investments should we make?" "How can we improve housing options?" and "How do we protect our community from natural disaster?"

Table 1. Requirements and Options Provided in G.S. 160D-501

Purpose	"A comprehensive or land-use plan is intended to guide coordinated, efficient, and orderly development within the planning and development regulation jurisdiction based on an analysis of present and future needs."	
Definition	"A comprehensive plan sets forth goals, policies, and programs intended to guide the present and future physical, social, and economic development of the jurisdiction."	"A land-use plan uses text and maps to designate the future use or reuse of land."
Data option	"Planning analysis may address inventories of existing conditions and assess future trends regarding demographics and economic, environmental, and cultural factors."	
Process requirement	"The planning process shall include opportunities for citizen engagement in plan preparation and adoption."	
Other plans	"A local government may prepare and adopt such other plans as deemed appropriate. This may include, but is not limited to, small area plans, neighborhood plans, hazard mitigation plans, transportation plans, housing plans, and recreation and open space plans."	
Adoption	"Plans shall be adopted by the governing board with the advice and consultation of the planning board. Adoption and amendment of a comprehensive plan is a legislative decision and shall follow the process mandated for zoning text amendments set by G.S. 160D-601."	
Relationship to other plans (such as county plans or CAMA plans)	"Plans adopted under this Chapter may be undertaken and adopted as part of or in conjunction with plans required under other statutes, including, but not limited to, the plans required by G.S. 113A-110." "A local government may undertake any of the planning activities authorized by this Article in coordination with other local governments, State agencies, or regional agencies created under Article 19 of Chapter 153A of the General Statutes or Article 20 of Chapter 160A of the General Statutes."	

Photos by Ben Hitchings.

In order to answer those big questions, a community must explore the underlying questions of current conditions, community priorities, best practices, and implementation options. To that end the planning process outlined in this guidebook is focused on land use planning, grounded in key data for current conditions and trends, guided by authentic community input, informed by planning best practices, and aligned with practical implementation strategies. Through that process and with an adopted plan, a local government can engage citizens in decision making, wisely invest public dollars, guide development decisions, qualify for certain grant and government funding, and more.

At the same time, the plan is one piece in a large puzzle of community success. It presents a vision for the future that requires additional action to be implemented, and it should reflect the community's particular values and priorities.

In addition to the good substantive reasons for local land use planning, North Carolina law requires that a local government must have a reasonably up-to-date land use plan or comprehensive plan in order to enforce land use zoning. In 2019, the N.C. General Assembly passed legislation that reorganized North Carolina's planning statutes into a new chapter of the N.C. General Statutes, Chapter 160D. The legislation also made a number of revisions to state planning statutes, most of which were minor updates. However, one significant policy change was a requirement that local governments adopt and maintain comprehensive plans or land use plans in order to retain their authority to adopt and apply zoning regulations. Communities have until July 1, 2022, to meet this requirement or risk losing their zoning authority. The table below summarizes requirements and options covered in G.S. 160D-501.

A Seven-Step Process

There are many ways to prepare a community plan. This guidebook describes a streamlined process for doing so based on best practices in the planning literature and the insights of experienced North Carolina practitioners. It includes seven key steps to drafting a plan that is both meaningful and efficient. Figure 1, a graphic of the process, is presented below.

Each of the seven steps is described in the pages that follow. The discussion of each step explains the *purpose* of that step, maps out a *timeline* for achieving it, summarizes *products* needed to succeed at the step, discusses *key considerations* related to the step, identifies *key tasks*, describes *other potential tasks* that might be accomplished if time and resources permit, provides *examples* from North Carolina communities, and lists additional *resources*. The guidebook takes this approach with the aim of assisting communities and planning service providers in preparing effective and cost-efficient plans that will help them address key opportunities and challenges and plan for a better future.

Figure 1. Seven Steps of Preparing a Community Plan

Step 1	Step 2	Step 3	Step 4	Step 5	Step 6	Step 7
Summarize Existing Conditions	Engage the Community	Set Goals and Policies	Map the Future	Select Implementation Strategies	Draft and Adopt the Plan	Move to Action

Substance of the Plan

The seven-step process helpfully guides a community through the tasks of comprehensive or land use planning. A key question remains: What is the substance of the plan? What are topics are to be addressed? North Carolina law does not require particular elements in a plan, but Chapter 160D includes suggested elements and planning best practices suggest certain elements. These substantive areas, listed below, are integrated throughout the guidebook's approach to planning—topics for data gathering, substance for engaging the community, categories for goals, and so on.

1. Natural Resources and Hazards

- Protection of natural attractions, agricultural resources, mineral resources, and water and air quality
- Mitigation of natural hazards such as flooding, high winds, wildfires, and unstable lands

2. Community Resources and Assets

- Architectural, scenic, cultural, historical, and archaeological resources
- Community facilities, including recreation facilities and open spaces
- Community health and health care

3. Community Development and Housing

- Community access to resources
- Existing land use patterns
- Range of available housing types and affordability of each type across resident income levels.

4. Economic Development

- Economic trends and outlook
- Employment opportunities
- Key economic sectors
- Ongoing economic development projects
- Opportunity sites and other economic assets (educational resources, etc.)

5. Public Facilities and Infrastructure

- Transportation facilities, including transit, roads, sidewalks, greenways, and bike facilities
- Infrastructure, including water, sewer, stormwater, and waste disposal
- Telecommunications and broadband internet infrastructure and availability
- Fiscal health and funding strategies
- Facilities and funding for public services, including emergency services and education

6. Future Development Patterns

- Location, distribution, and characteristics of future land uses, urban form, utilities, and transportation networks

Does Our Plan Need an Update?

If your local government has an adopted a comprehensive plan or land use plan, how do you know whether it should be updated? Both legal and practical considerations factor into making this evaluation.

Chapter 160D, Section 501 of the N.C. General Statutes (hereinafter G.S.) states that North Carolina law requires that local governments "adopt and reasonably maintain a comprehensive plan or land use plan" as a condition of "adopting and applying zoning regulations." However, the statutes do not specifically define the term "reasonably maintain." In general, professional practice calls for community plans to be updated every five to ten years. If the community has experienced limited change, then a plan that was adopted up to ten years ago might still be useful. If the community has experienced rapid change, then an update every five years may be more defensible. If the plan has been in place for several decades, though, it is probably time to update it.

Photos by Ben Hitchings.

Factors determining the frequency of plan updates include rate of growth and change as well as physical, economic, and social conditions. Also, keep in mind that the state requirement is for reasonable *maintenance*. There is no mandate for a complete rewrite of a community's comprehensive plan. As a point of reference, under prior law, land use plans for jurisdictions in the twenty "coastal" counties covered by the Coastal Area Management Act (CAMA) were required to be updated every five years.

Does Our Community Really Have to Create a Plan?

There are many good reasons that a community may want to establish a land use or comprehensive plan, but it is not necessary or appropriate for every community to take on planning and zoning alone. The resources required for crafting and maintaining a plan can be substantial, and the administration of land development regulations is no small task. Before beginning the planning process, a community should first identify the community needs and priorities, confirm the requirements for planning and zoning, and assess town resources. If a town wants to have and enforce its own zoning, the town will need to adopt and maintain a land use plan, but there are many alternatives to consider.

The following questions will help a community determine if they should proceed with planning and zoning on their own or consider alternatives:

- Does the community have interest in guiding growth and development? What are the community's priorities related to growth and development? Planning and zoning is one way to guide growth, but it is not the only way and may not be the appropriate tool for a particular community.
- What is the current and projected volume of zoning requests and development proposals in the community? If there is limited projected growth, there may be less need for town-specific zoning.
- Does the community have the staff capacity to administer planning and zoning regulations? If not, does it have the financial resources to hire out for administration of planning and zoning regulations? Resources and capacity are key questions for implementation of any plan.
- Are there opportunities for the community to partner with the county in which it is situated, its regional council of government, or others to complete a plan and/or administer development standards? As discussed below, there are many alternatives for managing planning and zoning.

Many alternative arrangements exist for a small town that cannot take on all of the necessary planning and zoning responsibilities alone. In such circumstances, before embarking on a planning effort the town should consider the following alternatives:

- Partner for joint planning. The town may coordinate planning efforts with the county, the regional council of governments, neighboring towns, or other entities.
- Partner to apply county zoning. The town may coordinate with the county to have county zoning enforced within the municipal limits.
- Remove zoning. If development volumes are low, the town may be able to rely on basic ordinances such as a flood-damage prevention ordinance, a high-impact industry ordinance, and/or a minimum-housing ordinance. Without the existence of zoning, there is no state requirement that the town must have a plan.

Once a community has determined whether it needs to develop a new plan or update an existing one, now it can begin the planning process. The rest of this book describes a seven-step process for doing this.

General Resources

Godschalk, David R., and William R. Anderson. *Sustaining Places: The Role of the Comprehensive Plan*. PAS Report 567. Chicago: American Planning Association, 2012. This report provides a useful overview of the value of the comprehensive plan in addressing community issues.

Godschalk, David R., and David C. Rouse. *Sustaining Places: Best Practices for Comprehensive Plans*. PAS Report 578. Chicago: American Planning Association, 2015. This report presents a framework for evaluating plans and an extensive listing of best practices for policies to include in them.

N.C. Division of Coastal Management. *N.C. CAMA Comprehensive Planning Guide*. Raleigh: N.C. Division of Coastal Management, 2021. This document lists a number of useful data sources for gathering background information on N.C. communities, presents a good introduction to the CAMA land use planning process, and includes a variety of best practices for policies communities can include in their plans.

Step 1: Summarize Existing Conditions

Purpose
The first step in the process of creating a community plan is to gather and analyze information about the existing conditions and emerging trends in the community. This information will help identify some of the advantages, assets, and challenges that tell a community's story. Establishing this fact base can also help build a shared understanding of where the community is and where it wants to go.

Timeline
This part of the planning process can take three to four weeks if data analysis efforts are focused.

Products
Common products at this stage of the planning process include narrative descriptions, tables, charts, maps, and infographics with summary statistics about the community.

Key Considerations
- Establishing a shared fact base is the first step to developing a shared vision.
- Make sure to present relevant information in a clear manner.
- Highlighting key takeaways from the data will go a long way toward understanding what the data can tell you about the status of the community and its needs.
- While the data review does not need to be exhaustive, it should provide a broad overview of existing conditions and, if possible, emerging trends. (Note that there may be an opportunity to do some additional analysis later in the process.)
- Inviting stakeholders to share information can yield valuable insights.
- Identify those attributes that most clearly paint an accurate picture of the community.

Key Tasks

Gather and present available community data. This task involves compiling and analyzing information about the community's population, economy, environmental features, land use patterns, infrastructure, and other characteristics. What are the distinguishing features of the community and its residents, and how are these features evolving? This guidebook includes a Sample Data Collection Plan (Template 1B) with links to online data sources that address these questions and more. The gathered data should establish baseline information and trends for suggested comprehensive-plan elements falling under the Natural Resources and Hazards, Community Resources and Assets, Community Development and Housing, Economic Development, and Public Facilities and Infrastructure categories identified earlier in this guidebook.

In some cases, limited data may be available at the municipal level, especially in small towns. In these cases, it may be possible to use county-level data as a proxy. If doing so, do so cautiously and check to see if the data seem generally applicable. In addition, the planning team can supplement available data with local knowledge from community stakeholders, who can often can provide valuable insights into local issues.

Review existing community plans. Examining and summarizing each of the community's relevant existing plans is important to developing a shared understanding of the current policy landscape and areas of agreement and inconsistency across these documents. The comprehensive plan or land use plan provides the community with an opportunity to harmonize its policy framework so that the various plans are not working at cross-purposes. Examples of related plans include a transportation plan, parks and recreation master plan, greenways master plan, economic development plan, housing or community development plan, hazard-mitigation plan, and capital improvements program. It may be helpful to create a simple matrix that summarizes the key policies from each plan and to highlight those policies that are consistent and inconsistent with each other. Prior plans (if readily available) can provide some insight into the community's history and prior development priorities.

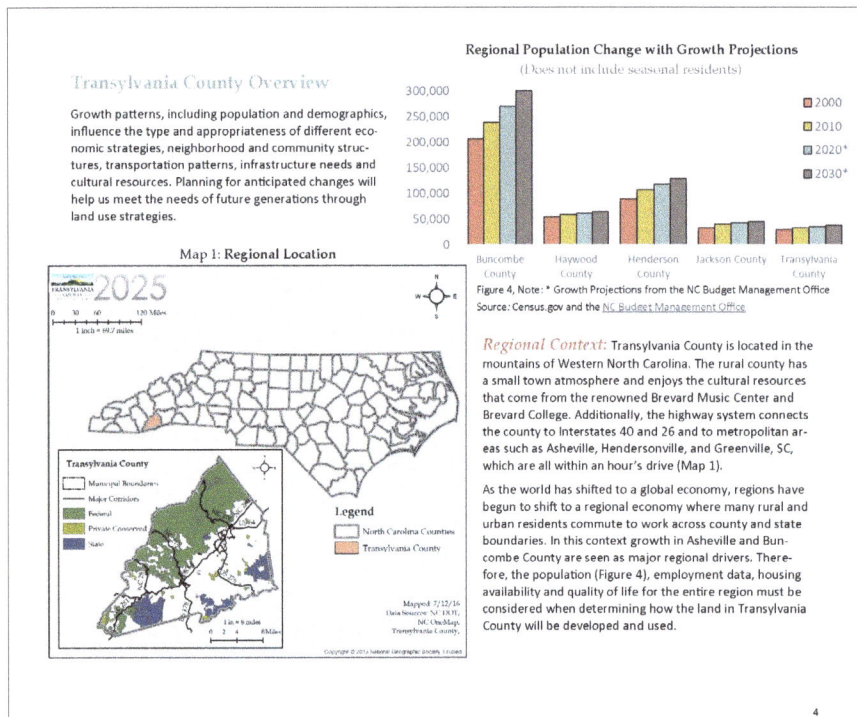

2025 Transylvania County Comprehensive Plan (2018), 4. Courtesy of Transylvania County.

Interview key stakeholders. If you are an outside consultant coming into a community to help its leaders prepare a plan, it is important to remember that there may be much you don't know about the community, including the current personalities and political dynamics as well as the specifics of local growth and development issues. Therefore, talking with a sampling of key officials at the outset of the planning project could be quite helpful to get a better sense of the main issues. Good people to talk with often include the community's mayor and planning board chair; the town manager; and other local leaders, such as clergy members, neighborhood leaders, non-profit staff, major employers, and chambers of commerce staff. Every community has its own context, and getting early insight into crucial issues can be helpful in ensuring a productive planning process. In addition, many of these individuals may represent formal or informal sponsors of the plan who can help make the planning process a success or failure and who will be evaluating the resulting product. Thus, capturing their insights and priorities at the start of the process is very important, especially when working with a compressed timeline. At the back of this guidebook, Templates 2B and 2C offer sample questions for initial discussions with local government staff and interview questions for key stakeholders.

Infographics showing community data and trends from *Grow Harnett County: Comprehensive Plan 2015*, 2. Courtesy of Harnett County.

Conduct a site tour of the community. This task is important to help the planning team get up to speed on the community, to familiarize themselves with where things are located, and to identify what the issues are. Touring the community with knowledgeable local guides, such as local government staff or officials, can expedite this process and help the planning team better understand the context that the plan needs to address. In addition, the tour provides a good opportunity to begin taking photos to use in presentations and to help illustrate the plan.

Draft a summary of existing conditions and emerging trends. This draft should be shared with key stakeholders and decision makers. It will serve as baseline data to be shared with community members as part of community engagement efforts, it may help to identify gaps in the initial data gathering, and it will serve as a first draft of the existing conditions portion of the land use plan.

Other Potential Tasks

If a community has the time and resources, it might consider conducting some or all of the additional tasks listed below as part of this step.

- **Prepare a series of background maps** to share important project information in an engaging and understandable way. For example, the *2016 Gaston County Comprehensive Plan* includes an extensive map series that shows environmental features, historic and cultural resources, water supply watershed areas, recreational resources, population distribution, and other applicable county features.
- **Review applicable county and regional plans** to help coordinate planning efforts across jurisdictional lines.
- **Conduct a market/economic analysis** to ground the plan in an understanding of market economics and to assess the market potential for private development and economic growth.
- **Prepare a land suitability analysis** to identify which parts of the community are most suitable for different land uses, such as agriculture, habitat conservation, and new development.
- **Prepare a population cohort analysis** showing the number of residents in various age ranges to better understand community population dynamics.
- **Conduct an emerging issues analysis** to better understand disruptive new trends and to prepare for drivers of change, such as an aging population, increased automation, and climate change.

Resources

The appendix includes a sample project timeline (Template 1A) and a worksheet for analyzing a community's existing conditions (Template 1B).

School of Government. *PlanNC Existing Conditions Manual*, supplement to the *PlanNC Guidebook*. Available on Canvas.

School of Government. *PlanNC Data Tables and Tutorials Cheat Sheet*, supplement to the *PlanNC Guidebook*. Available on Canvas.

Step 2: Engage the Community

Purpose

The second step in the process of creating a community plan is to engage stakeholders in the community. Our goal is not just to inform and educate ourselves and the community, but also to involve, learn from, and empower community stakeholders to help shape the decisions that affect them and their fellow citizens. This engagement not only provides valuable input into the plan but can build a sense of ownership and buy-in from the community. If community members feel that they have helped to shape their plan, they may be more motivated to pursue implementation of that plan. Full engagement can also help to mitigate controversies that arise later around the plan's policies.

Timeline

The public involvement phase is often the longest and most time-consuming step in the planning process. This guidebook allocates eight to thirteen weeks for communities and service providers to complete community-engagement work. This is a compressed time frame compared to most plan-development processes, but it nevertheless should strike the necessary balance between giving enough time to engage the diversity of stakeholders in the community and keeping the process moving.

Products

Potential products to use at the engagement phase include public-input summaries and data on the extent of outreach efforts and the level of community engagement in the planning process. These summaries may include meeting notes, written submissions, or files of quantitative data. This input is vital to informing the goal-setting and plan-drafting stages that will come next.

Key Considerations

- Public involvement is an essential part of creating a comprehensive plan or land use plan; in fact, G.S. 160D-501(a) *requires* that opportunities for citizen engagement be provided in the planning process.
- Set appropriate expectations; be clear about the scope of the planning topics and process and establish practical implementation strategies for land use planning.

- Public engagement allows stakeholders to share insights and aspirations for the community, facilitates a shared vision for the future of the community, and builds stakeholder investment in the plan.
- Silence does not always mean agreement, so finding ways to draw people out to say what they think is important.
- Track input so that it can be reflected in the process and the plan. The community input step of the process can provide many ideas and good direction for later steps in the process. In addition, tracking participation as you go can help in identifying groups that have not yet been involved so that subsequent outreach efforts can work to involve them in the planning process.
- Robust and authentic engagement throughout the planning process can protect against last-minute claims that the public was never told about the plan.
- Strong public engagement can build good will, help create planning champions, and establish a base of support that helps move the community forward in the months and years ahead.
- Public engagement may require more than just a couple of open meetings; find opportunities to meet community members where they are (e.g., at community events, major employment centers, etc.).

Key Tasks

Draft a short public-involvement plan to outline how you are going to engage the various stakeholders in the community, including both the ones who commonly participate in community decisions and the ones who may be harder to reach. The process of drafting a short public-involvement plan provides an opportunity to think through techniques that (1) would be most effective for engaging a range of stakeholders in your community and (2) are also feasible, given project resources. After finishing this draft, you can map out the techniques you identified on a timeline and pinpoint key tasks needed to make them happen. The public-involvement plan should include ways to gather public input on the opportunities and challenges related to suggested comprehensive-plan elements falling under the Natural Resources and Hazards, Community Resources and Assets,

Sample public meeting announcements for *Our Town Belmont: Comprehensive Blueprint for Our Future* (2018). Courtesy of the Town of Belmont.

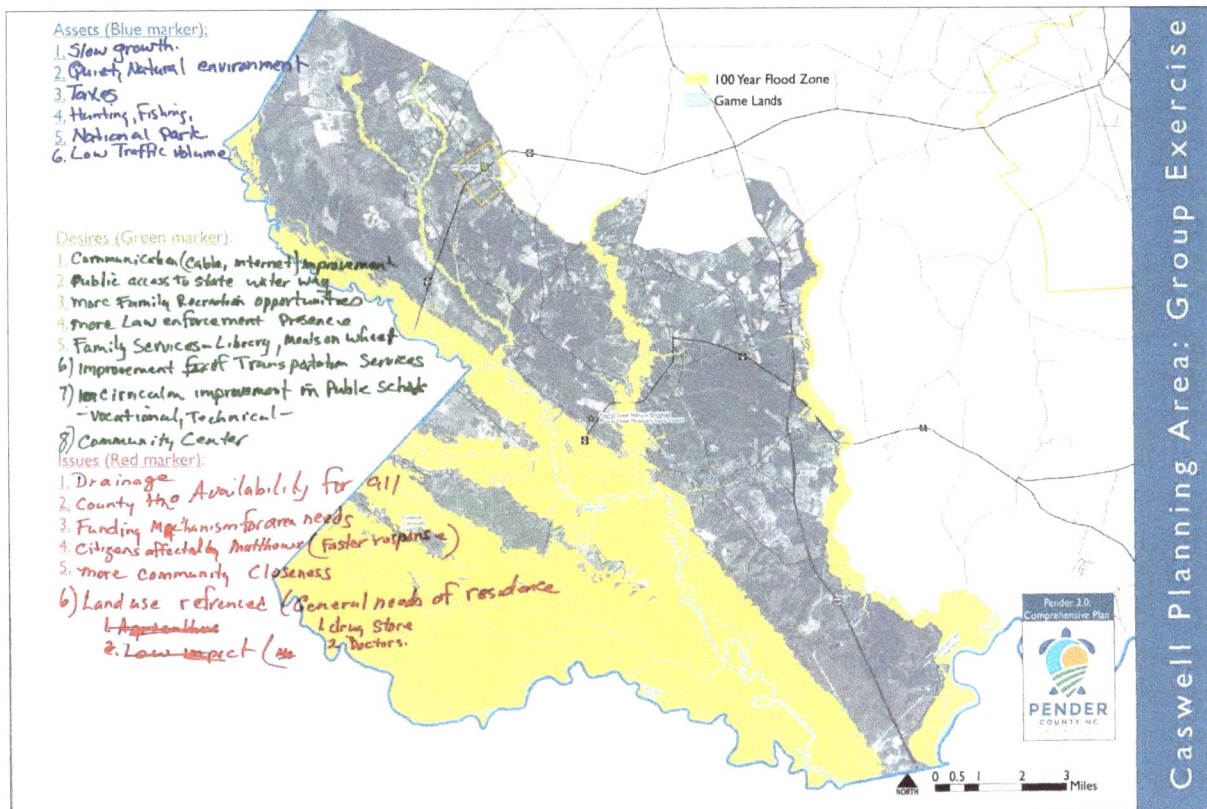

Marked-up map with public comments received by Pender County. Reprinted with permission from Pender County, *Pender County 2.0 Comprehensive Land Use Plan* (2018), Appendix C.

Community Development and Housing, Economic Development, and Public Facilities and Infrastructure categories identified earlier in this guidebook. The public-involvement plan should also include outreach efforts that are accessible to all members of the community, including those with limited internet access, reduced mobility, or challenging work hours. At the back of this guide, Template 2A walks through the preparation of a customized public engagement plan.

Create a web page and links to provide project information, a project timeline, and updates on public-involvement opportunities. As online engagement has become widespread, there is often an expectation that community-planning projects will have an online presence. You could create a page on the existing community website or a stand-alone website. As a rule, it is helpful to keep the web page simple and easy to navigate. Keeping it updated helps give stakeholders a reason to come back to it and also helps demonstrate the progress being made on the project. More-extensive websites could provide a comment box, a platform for posting flash polls of engaging community questions, and an opportunity for hosting activities like a photo contest of places people like in the community. If the local government doesn't have a web page sometimes other online platforms can be used instead, such as a Facebook page or Twitter or Instagram account.

Hold community workshops, whether in person, online, or both, to share information about the planning project and to receive public input. Workshops provide opportunities to engage stakeholders through various activities. The best ones often provide multiple formats for providing input, including verbal, written, and electronic opportunities, recognizing that different stakeholders may feel more comfortable offering comments and questions in different ways. Workshops also present an opportunity to harness the power of fun to engage stakeholders. For example, a community with a railroad history

Sample survey results from the Town of Black Mountain (left) and sample word cloud showing input received by the City of Clinton (right). Reprinted with permission from Town of Black Mountain, *2014 Comprehensive Plan Update for the Town of Black Mountain*, A-2; and City of Clinton, *City of Clinton 2035 Comprehensive Plan* (2015), 7-14.

might distribute a special train ticket to each workshop participant as they enter the meeting room and then punch the ticket as they visit each of several information stations. Then, any participants who have visited all the stations could be entered into a drawing held at the end of the workshop session and be eligible to win fabulous prizes.

Another key element is providing engaging visuals. A workshop might include a community map that asks participants to identify where they live, what common destinations they visit, and what their favorite places are in the community. Another technique is to conduct a community preference survey that asks workshop participants to rate their preferences for different kinds of places using sample photos, with the results being used to inform plan goals and objectives. Template 2D offers a sample agenda for a community workshop.

Hold open houses to provide project information and create a more informal opportunity for stakeholders to share input and ask questions. Open houses often start with a short presentation and then invite stakeholders to view posters displayed at information stations staffed by community planners and project consultants. One efficient approach is to pair an open house with a regular meeting of a planning board or governing board. People can attend the open house to get some background on a project and to ask questions, and then they can listen to a formal presentation on the project at the ensuing board meeting.

Conduct public hearings to give stakeholders an opportunity to provide comments on the planning project to appointed and elected board members. G.S. Chapter 160D requires that local governments adopt plans using the same process as is used for zoning text amendments, which means sending the proposed plan (1) to the planning board for review and recommendation and then (2) to the governing board for review and adoption. In addition, the governing board must hold a legislative hearing to provide a more formal opportunity for stakeholders to comment on the proposed plan. Holding a less-formal open

Forms of Public Participation

Many planners are familiar with Sherry Arnstein's famous Ladder of Participation. The International Association of Public Participation (IAP2) has prepared its own version that includes the following five stages:

Inform. Provide balanced and objective information to assist the public in understanding the problem, alternatives, opportunities, and/or solutions; examples include infographics, fact sheets, websites, open houses, mailings, and social media posts.

Consult. Obtain public feedback on analysis, alternatives, and/or decisions; examples include public comment periods, focus groups, surveys, and public meetings.

Involve. Work directly with the public throughout the process to ensure that public concerns and aspirations are consistently understood and considered; examples include workshops and deliberative polling.

Collaborate. Partner with the public in each aspect of the decision, including the development of alternatives and the identification of the preferred solution; examples include stakeholder advisory committees, consensus-building activities, and participatory decision making.

Empower. Place final decision making in the hands of the public; examples include stakeholder juries, resident boards, public referenda, and delegated decisions.

Source: Adapted from the City of Raleigh's *Public Participation Playbook* (2020), p.11.

house immediately prior to the board hearing can help to answer stakeholders' questions outside the bright lights of the meeting room and help interested participants to provide more appropriate comments at the board meeting. Adding a public hearing on top of the planning board's review meeting can also help identify concerns or items needing further discussion before the plan is up for approval. Template 2E offers a sample plan progress report for planning and governing boards.

Other Potential Tasks

- Staff a table and **hold pop-up activities** at regularly scheduled community festivals and events to engage stakeholders in the planning process.
- **Hold on-site meetings** to meet people where they are, such as at churches or at regularly scheduled neighborhood meetings, to engage them about the planning project. This can provide one of the best ways to engage hard-to-reach stakeholders by making it convenient for them to participate, and it also communicates the importance that the project team places on their participation.
- **Lead focus groups** to explore particular topics in greater depth with specific groups of stakeholders, such as senior citizens, farmers, or small-business people.
- **Coordinate with local media outlets** to broadcast your message and advertise your events.
- **Launch a social media strategy** to provide regular plan updates and publicize special activities.
- **Write a regular blog** to answer common questions or share information on special topics.
- **Conduct live polling** using smart phones or special keypads to gather input quickly and anonymously from large groups.

- **Conduct paper or online surveys** to gather input from large groups of people, some of whom may not have the time to attend live events.
- **Create an interactive project website** where you can post plan-progress reports, flash polls, online surveys, and other information and activities to help engage stakeholders in the planning process.
- **Designate neighborhood ambassadors** who can spread the word about the planning initiative and let people know about various public-input opportunities.
- **Hold in-person or online contests** to create a sense of fun and excitement and help engage stakeholders. Select some contest winners randomly from a given group, such as attendees at the community-planning workshop. Other contests can be competitive; for example, invite stakeholders to make a piece of art celebrating the community or to share a photo of their favorite place in the community.
- Invite stakeholders to **share stories** about the history of their community or about life in the community. This is a compelling way to highlight opportunities and challenges and to identify things that people love or want to change in their community. These sharing sessions could be recorded in short video segments, perhaps during a community workshop, and posted on the planning-project website or spliced into a summary video to show at a public event.
- Distribute a **"meeting in a box"** to provide a self-serve tool for engaging stakeholders. As part of this activity, assemble and distribute a "to-go" kit of information and activities, perhaps including a small guide or the relevant meeting agenda. This is a great way to involve neighborhood ambassadors, who might be charged with leading a meeting in their part of the community and then reporting back the results.
- **Film short videos** and share them on the planning-project website. A series of short videos over the course of the planning process can serve as regular project updates or overviews of key topics.
- **Create story maps or interactive mapping**, both of which are highly visual ways to share information about the planning project or key planning topics.
- **Hold a speaker series on plan topics** to bring in outside expertise, introduce new ideas, and prepare the community for the planning process.
- **Develop project branding**, such as a project logo and tagline, to increase stakeholder awareness of the project. While creating a special logo can require design expertise, it is often relatively easy to come up with a name for the project. Below are some examples.

  - *Our Town Belmont: Comprehensive Blueprint for the Future*
  - *Plan Chatham: Working Together to Preserve and Progress*
  - *Clemmons Community Compass: 2040 Comprehensive Plan*
  - *Pender 2.0: Comprehensive Land Use Plan*
  - *Stokes County 2035: Moving Together*
  - *2013–2023 Comprehensive Plan, Washington, NC: Pride in the Past, Faith in the Future*

Resources

The appendix contains worksheets and guidelines for planning community-engagement work (Template 2A), sample interview questions for staff members and stakeholders (Templates 2B and 2C), a sample agenda for a community workshop (2D), and scripts for reporting progress to a governing board's staff and elected officials (2E).

American Planning Association's (APA) "Knowledgebase" on online public engagement, https://www .planning.org/knowledgebase/onlineengagement/ (note: one must be an APA member to access this site).

Davenport Institute. Online public engagement hub. https://publicpolicy.pepperdine.edu /davenport-institute/thought-leadership/news.htm.

Herd, Milton J. *A Planner's Guide to Meeting Facilitation.* PAS Report 595. Chicago: APA, 2019. https://www.planning.org/publications/report/9178119/ (note: one must be an APA member to access this site).

International Association of Public Participation official website. http://www.iap2.org.

Kaner, Sam. *Facilitator's Guide to Participatory Decision-Making.* 3rd ed. Hoboken, N.J.: Jossey-Bass, 2014.

Public Participation Partners. *Community Engagement Process Development: Public Participation Playbook.* Raleigh: Public Participation Partners, 2020. https://cityofraleigh0drupal.blob.core.usgovcloudapi .net/drupal-prod/COR22/CEPDPlaybook.pdf.

State of California. "Community Engagement and Outreach: Designing Healthy, Equitable, Resilient, and Economically Vibrant Places." https://opr.ca.gov/docs/OPR_C3_final.pdf.

Step 3: Set Goals and Policies

Purpose

The purpose of Step 3 is to use the data obtained in Step 1 and the public input received in Step 2 to help craft goals and policies for the community. Together, these goal and policy statements will describe a shared vision for how the community will use land and develop its transportation network and other systems in the years ahead.

Timeline

If possible, try to conduct this step in three to four weeks to keep the planning process moving and to provide timely follow-up on the initial public input received.

Products

The key products for successfully completing this step are the draft goals and policies that will be shared with boards, key stakeholders, and the community, leading up to their inclusion in the community plan.

Key Considerations

- By synthesizing public input, you ensure that the community's voice is shaping the specific goals and overall policy of the plan.
- Draft goals and policies can match community desires for the future with actionable strategies to move toward that future.
- Once the draft goals and policies have been prepared, it is important to share them in preliminary form with community stakeholders through the planning-project website, an open house or community meeting, and/or board presentations.

Key Tasks

Synthesize public input to capture recurring comments and identify key themes. What do people love about the community that they want to protect and preserve? What outstanding issues or challenges need to be addressed? What do they want to change about the community or add to it? Do the public comments suggest an overall vision for the future? A key aspect of the work in Step 3 involves showing stakeholders that you are listening and considering the input they have provided. One way to do this is to document every piece of input received and then draft a response for how that input will or will not be addressed in the plan. This could be done in summary form to share the main comments received and the major themes emphasized. Be advised that many stakeholders will check to see whether their comments have been captured and considered. Template 3A outlines an approach to synthesizing public input.

Draft high-level goals and more-detailed policies to include in the plan, drawing on the stakeholder input received. Every planning process combines public input with professional expertise. Community stakeholders are experts on what they and their communities want. The planning-project team has an important role to play in helping stakeholders understand the implications of different actions and in charting a workable way to help the community move toward its desired vision. This step involves drafting both goals and policies for the community to achieve by implementing the plan. Goals are aspects of the community's vision of its ideal future; they are descriptive and use mostly nouns and adjectives. Example goals include "a vibrant downtown," "an adequate supply of affordable housing," or "adequate park space." Policies are more-specific, measurable, concrete, and often time-bound outcomes that the community would like to achieve in implementing the plan; they are action-oriented and use mostly verbs and nouns. Example policies include "attract new businesses to downtown," "increase the stock of housing that is affordable to median income families," "establish five new small parks in the next five years," or "establish an economic development corporation." Goals and policies may be organized under the following categories, identified earlier in this guidebook in the discussion of comprehensive-plan elements.

- Natural Resources and Hazards
- Community Resources and Assets
- Community Development and Housing
- Economic Development
- Public Facilities and Infrastructure
- Future Development Patterns

Template 3B is a worksheet to help guide the drafting of goals and policies.

Share draft goals and policies with key stakeholders and decision makers to gather feedback and allow for refinement of the drafts. It can be helpful to present the draft goals and policies with statements as basic as, "This is what we heard. Did we get it right? What revisions should we make?" Often, it is easier to reach agreement on the goals, since they are more general than the policies. Draft policies and actions might stir up more debate as terms and descriptions become more specific, specific actions are proposed, and stakeholders begin to form perceptions regarding the trade-offs, who will benefit, and who will lose out. As a result, it is important to listen carefully to stakeholders' comments and concerns to understand their underlying interests, identify ways to mitigate potential detrimental impacts, and create win-win situations.

Other Potential Tasks

Conduct additional analysis to explore in more depth the current conditions, challenges, and opportunities related to particular plan topics, such as health or utilities, that were raised in public comment sessions but not addressed by the data gathered in Step 1.

Examples

- The following excerpts from recent North Carolina plans can serve as examples of how your community might consider drafting and organizing its overarching goals.

Plan Chatham | COMPREHENSIVE REPORT

GOALS

The vision is supported by a set of interrelated goals that served as guideposts in the development of the plan. Going forward, the goals provide direction for County leaders as they make decisions about future development, conservation, and related investments over the next two decades. The matrix below shows the relationship of the goals to the 10 plan elements, indicating that achievement of a goal ensures progress on two or more plan elements.

GOAL

1. Preserve the rural character and lifestyle of Chatham County.

2. Preserve, protect, and enable agriculture and forestry.

3. Promote a compact growth pattern by developing in and near existing towns, communities, and in designated, well planned, walkable, mixed use centers.

4. Diversify the tax base and generate more quality, in-county jobs to reduce dependence on residential property taxes, create economic opportunity and reduce out-commuting.

5. Conserve natural resources.

6. Provide recreational opportunities and access to open space.

7. Provide infrastructure to support desired development and support economic and environmental objectives.

8. Become more resilient by mitigating, responding and adapting to emerging threats.

9. Provide equitable access to high-quality education, housing and community options for all.

10. Foster a healthy community.

40

Sample goals from the *Plan Chatham Comprehensive Plan* (2017). Courtesy of Chatham County.

Clinton 2035 Comprehensive Plan

C. Goals

The following twelve (12) goals have been heavily influenced by public input/opinion received during the planning process (see Section 7.B, Public Input). An annual review of these goals should be conducted by the City Council and Planning Board, and adjusted, if necessary, as implementation is accomplished. These goals are interrelated and, therefore, are not prioritized.

- *Goal 1.* In all decisions/actions, Clinton will consider the impact on Clinton's future as a progressive, welcoming, and stable community.

- *Goal 2.* Clinton will emphasize involvement of its citizens in its decision making processes.

- *Goal 3.* Clinton will focus on improving recreation/entertainment opportunities with an emphasis on activities for youth and active living.

- *Goal 4.* Clinton will emphasize preservation of the Downtown area through small business entrepreneurship including arts/cultural activities.

- *Goal 5.* Clinton will continue efforts to diversify job opportunities with an emphasis on "high technology" job opportunities.

- *Goal 6.* Clinton will vigorously support continued development of its health services industry.

- *Goal 7.* Clinton will, through its land development ordinance, provide an inventory of options for industrial/business development.

- *Goal 8.* Clinton will consider preservation of residential neighborhoods in its decision making processes.

- *Goal 9.* Clinton will support infill development as an action essential to the continued development of the city.

- *Goal 10.* Clinton will continuously support improvement of the educational systems serving the City.

- *Goal 11.* Clinton will support improvements to its infrastructure systems, including improvement of its regional access and access management.

- *Goal 12.* Clinton will support the improvement of health disparate neighborhoods, including emphasis on active living and access to healthy food options.

Sample goals from the *Clinton 2035 Comprehensive Plan (2015).* Courtesy of the City of Clinton.

Resources

Plans from other communities provide numerous examples of goals and policies. Look to these plans for guidance but at the same time make sure to respond to the public input provided by your community and to customize the goals and policies to that community.

The appendix contains worksheets for synthesizing input from the public (Template 3A) and developing goals (Template 3B).

Step 4: Map the Future

Purpose

Step 4 is designed to map the goals and policies established in Step 3 across the planning jurisdiction, leading to a proposed future land use pattern that will help implement the community's shared vision. The product that usually results from this work is a Future Land Use Map (FLUM) that is often included in the plan.

Timeline

This step can take four to nine weeks, depending on how much analysis is involved and whether the community has ready access to mapping expertise.

Products

Key products to be used in this step include a table and descriptions of the future land use categories, as well as a FLUM. More extensive work may generate "scenario analysis" to measure the relative community benefits of different approaches to future land use.

Key Considerations

- Bear in mind that it is easy to get bogged down in this step because of the range and detail of potential analyses that can be conducted.
- At the end of the day, the most important tasks are conducting the "change analysis" and preparing the FLUM, so focusing on these tasks can help move this step forward in a timely manner.
- It is often helpful to describe different land uses as "place types" that help the average person understand what they are, such as by saying "main street commercial development" instead of "high-density, mixed-use commercial."
- It is important to be cognizant that proposing changes in land use can be a controversial topic. One person's blight can be another person's home. As a result, look for sensitive ways to discuss it.
- Testing drafts of the future land use categories and map with stakeholders is essential to building a shared vision that reflects community preferences.

- Finding quality, affordable mapping assistance is key to successfully completing this step. If your community does not have GIS and mapping expertise and tools, perhaps your planning colleagues at the county, at the regional council of government, or at another potential service provider do.

Key Tasks

Conduct a change analysis to begin the process of mapping the goals and policies in the plan. To do this, work with community stakeholders to build agreement on places that should change in order to advance community goals and on places that should stay the same or be enhanced. Capturing stakeholder ideas on base maps during the public-involvement phase of the project can be a great way to help inform this task.

The product that results from this work is sometimes called a "growth strategy," which provides a broad-brush vision for how land should be used in the years ahead, with some areas identified for preservation, others identified for enhancement, and still others envisioned as future centers of activity. Conducting this step first (before preparing a FLUM) can help you manage the politics of change by taking the places that are slated to stay the same out of the equation, allaying the fears of stakeholders who want that continuity.

Template 4A offers additional guidance on crafting a change analysis.

Create a FLUM to (1) identify types of places or future land use categories throughout the community, (2) describe those places, and (3) map them. This work can build on the change analysis to identify the kinds of land uses that are desirable for the areas of change. The resulting FLUM displays the kinds of activities the community would like to see occur in the years ahead as well as where they would like to see them occur. One approach is to combine the change analysis and the FLUM development process, seeking input from stakeholders first on the one product and then on the other in the same meeting, then using the resulting input, along with professional expertise, to prepare a draft FLUM for review and comment by the community. Examples of different ways to identify and describe the range of land uses and places in a community include the new-urban transect ("The Transect," New Urban Network, n.d.) and the Triangle CommunityViz Development Patterns and Place Types Wheel (see page 4 of the *Triangle CommunityViz 2.0 Overview, 2016*).

Other Potential Tasks

- **Prepare more-detailed design concepts for key areas** to test and fine-tune the land use mix and give community stakeholders a better sense of the activities and land use design for these locations. This can be done with static images that are drawn by hand or rendered electronically, or through the creation of 3-D models that can support perspective views as well as virtual walk-throughs and fly-throughs. These activities require design and drawing or 3-D modeling skills and can be expensive, but they also can provide great visuals and a clearer sense of what is envisioned for key places in the community. Sometimes this work can be accomplished at minimal cost by using graduate design students.
- **Conduct scenario analysis** to give stakeholders a better sense of how different future land use scenarios might perform with regard to advancing community goals. A detailed version of this approach could involve conducting a land capacity analysis to see the extent to which different scenarios would contribute to the supply of land for various uses, as well as a systems analysis to evaluate the impact that the different scenarios have on community systems such as transportation and water and sewer service.

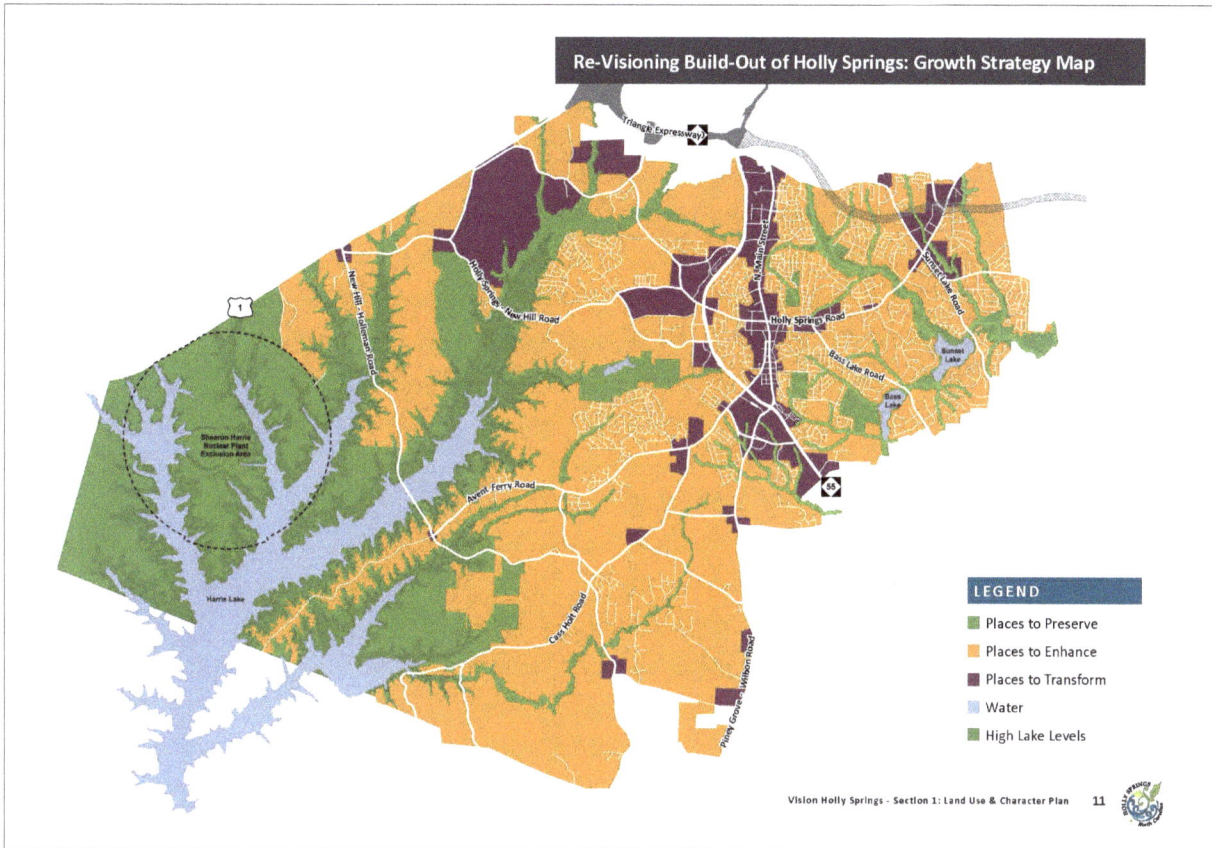

Re-Visioning Build-Out of Holly Springs: Growth Strategy Map

LEGEND
- Places to Preserve
- Places to Enhance
- Places to Transform
- Water
- High Lake Levels

Vision Holly Springs - Section 1: Land Use & Character Plan   11

This example of a change analysis from Holly Springs, N.C., identifies three basic types of places: places to preserve (like natural areas and historic sites), places to enhance (like existing residential areas), and places to transform (like aging commercial corridors or designated growth areas). *Holly Springs Comprehensive Plan, Land Use & Character Plan* (2019). Courtesy of the Town of Holly Springs.

Camden County
The 2035 Comprehensive Plan

Table 3: Future Land Use Designations

Future Land Use Designations			
Future Land Use	Residential Density	Land Uses	Wastewater Service
Environmental Preservation	n/a	Protected lands Dismal Swamp / North River Gamelands	Private wastewater
Rural Preservation	Max 1 dwelling unit per 5 acres	Very low density residential Farms and support uses Forestry and mining Environmentally sensitive lands	Private wastewater
Rural Residential	Max 1 dwelling unit per 1 acre	Low density residential Open space / recreation Public uses	Private wastewater
Village Residential	Max 3 dwelling units per 1 acre	Moderate density residential Open space / recreation Public uses	Public sanitary sewer appropriate
Village Mixed-Use	Range 3-14 dwelling units per 1 acre	Mix of residential uses Neighborhood serving commercial Open space / recreation Public uses	Public sanitary sewer appropriate
Village Center	Predominantly commercial (up to 14 dwelling units per 1 acre)	Village commercial/office Live/work units Public spaces / recreation Public uses	Public sanitary sewer appropriate
Village Commercial	n/a	Community commercial Professional offices Grocery/pharmacy Regional retail Open space/recreation Public uses	Public sanitary sewer appropriate
Village Commercial Corridor	n/a	Community commercial Professional offices Grocery/pharmacy Regional retail Open space/recreation Public uses	Public sanitary sewer appropriate
Crossroads Commercial	n/a	Rural commercial Open space/recreation Public uses	Private wastewater
Mixed-Use Employment	n/a	Business parks Research and development offices Industrial Commercial serving employment uses	Public sanitary sewer appropriate
Marine Commercial	n/a	Marinas Commercial fishing Marina serving retail/commercial	Private wastewater

The above table and following map from the *Camden County 2035 Comprehensive Plan* (2012), 39–40, show the progression of identifying place types or future land use categories throughout the community, describing these places, and mapping them. Courtesy of Camden County.

Step 4: Map the Future

Future Land Use

Camden County
The 2035 Comprehensive Plan

CLARION
October 2012

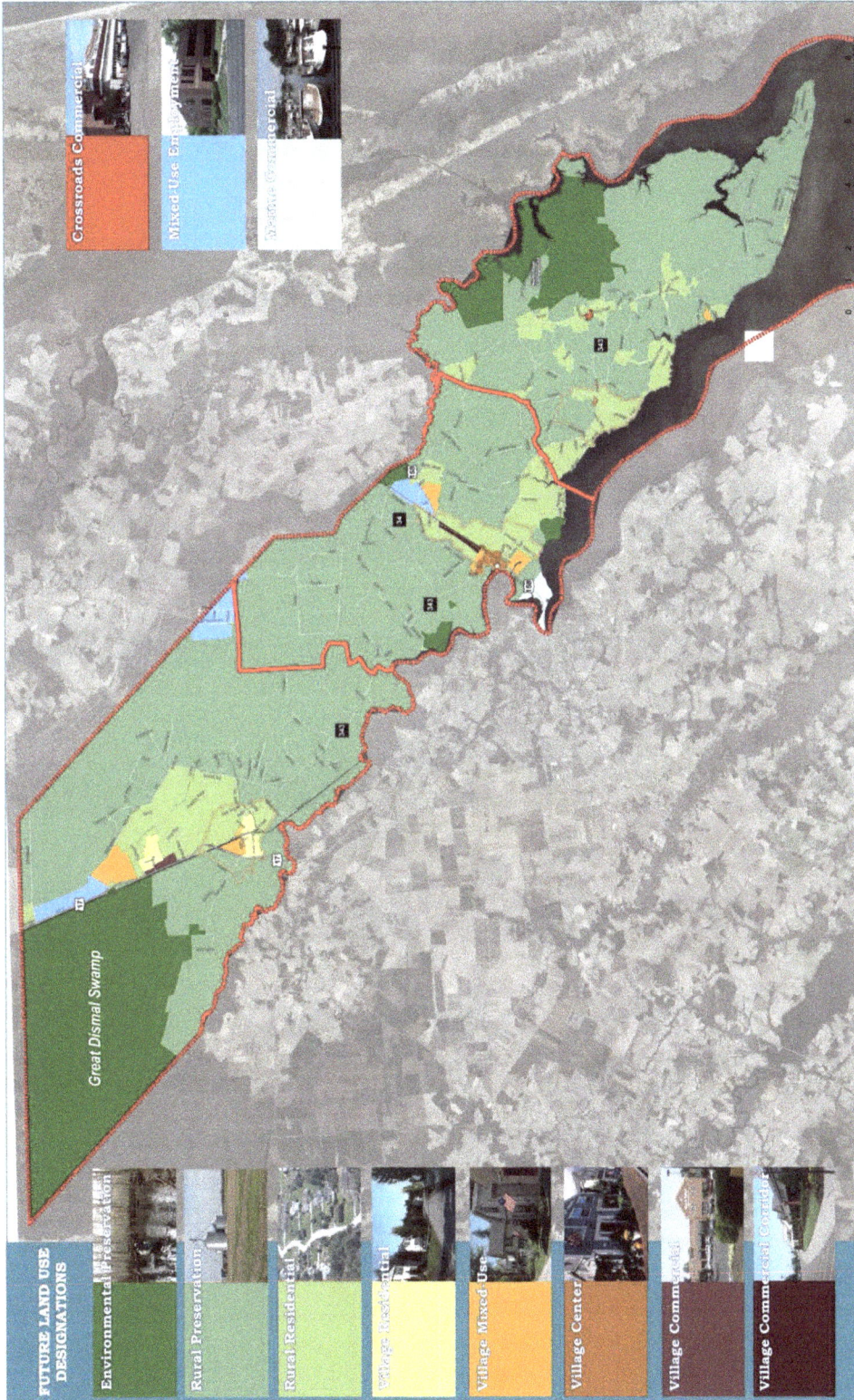

FUTURE LAND USE DESIGNATIONS

- Environmental Preservation
- Rural Preservation
- Rural Residential
- Village Residential
- Village Mixed Use
- Village Center
- Village Commercial
- Village Commercial Corridor

- Crossroads Commercial
- Mixed-Use Employment
- Productive Commercial

Great Dismal Swamp

Resources

The appendix contains a checklist for creating a FLUM (Template 4A).

Berke, Philip R., David R. Godschalk, and Edward J. Kaiser, with Daniel A. Rodriguez. "Designing the Spatial Arrangement of Land Uses." Chap. 10 in *Urban Land Use Planning.* 5th ed. Urbana: University of Illinois Press, 2006.

Futrell, Janae. *How to Design Your Scenario Planning Process*. PAS Memo July/August 2019. Chicago: American Planning Association, 2019.

McDaniel, Philip. "Getting started with QGIS." University of North Carolina at Chapel Hill, June 2021. Available on Canvas.

Miskowiak, Douglas. *Citizen's Guide to Future Land Use Mapping*. Stevens Point: University of Wisconsin–Stevens Point, 2006. https://www.uwsp.edu/cnr-ap/clue/Documents/DataMappingGIS/Citizen_Guide_Future_Land_Use_Mapping.pdf.

Oregon Department of Transportation and Oregon Department of Land Conservation and Development. *Oregon Scenario Planning Guidelines: Resources for Developing and Evaluating Alternative Land Use and Transportation Scenarios*. Salem: Oregon Department of Transportation, 2017. https://www.oregon.gov/ODOT/Planning/Documents/Oregon-Scenario-Planning-Guidelines.pdf.

Stapleton, Jeremy. *How to Use Exploratory Scenario Planning (XSP): Navigating an Uncertain Future*. Policy Focus Reports. Cambridge, Mass.: Lincoln Institute of Land Policy, 2020.

Step 5: Select Implementation Strategies

Purpose
The purpose of Step 5 is to identify potential plan-implementation strategies and select the ones best suited to advancing the community's shared vision.

Timeline
This step can take three to four weeks and sometimes longer, depending on the level of public involvement and whether the planning-project staff conduct a more-detailed implementation feasibility assessment to evaluate which projects are best suited to advancing community goals in a feasible manner.

Products
Key products to use during this step include a table of recommended implementation projects, along with information about each suggested measure; a responsible person or persons designated for each project; and a summary explaining why some projects were selected and others were not. A technical memo explaining the results of an implementation feasibility assessment may also be prepared.

Key Considerations
- Inviting stakeholder input on implementation strategies and sharing a draft list of measures with these stakeholders is important to build an effective portfolio that is supported by the community.
- Because of the tendency to list more projects than a community can readily implement, it is helpful to work with stakeholders and decision makers to prioritize a handful of measures for action. Reference to the goals identified in Step 3 can help to clarify priorities. Limiting the number of proposed measures can shift the focus to implementation efforts and build agreement on where to start.

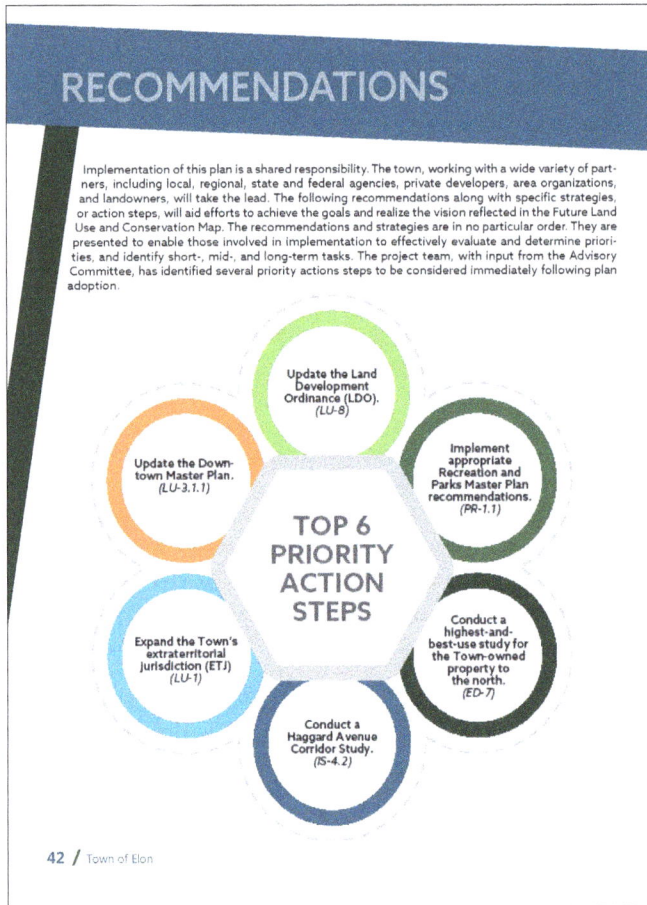

This page from the *Envision Elon 2040: Town of Elon Future Comprehensive Land Use Plan* (2019) provides a good example of identifying a manageable number of priority recommendations to help implement a plan. Courtesy of the Town of Elon.

Key Tasks

The first task is to **identify potential implementation strategies.** To do this, we often start by drawing from the general toolbox available to local governments, which includes development standards, public investments, programs, and partnerships. What strategies known to us and to others seem promising in helping the community implement the new plan? Below are some of the items in the toolbox.

- *Review local policies, regulations and jurisdiction*. Align development ordinances and other regulations with the priorities of the community plan. Align extraterritorial jurisdiction and annexation policies with the priorities of the plan.
- *Align the town government organization*. Organize local departments and staff to align with plan priorities and hire and train new staff to support the plan's success.
- *Focus town finances. Incorporate the plan into the annual budget process. Align the capital improvement plan with the comprehensive plan.* Seek public and grant funds to implement priority investments in parks, water and sewer services, trails, sidewalks, bike lanes, roads, and more.
- *Enhance community resources*. Maintain existing community assets (e.g., resources, businesses, housing); Recruit businesses and developments that align with the plan.
- *Build partnerships*. Align your planning efforts with the business community, nonprofits, the county, state agencies, and others.
- *Public outreach and education*. Educate the community about plan elements and priorities; maintain public engagement.

just require other actions to be completed first, whether stated in this Plan or not, to be possible, effective, or necessary.

ACTIONS (BY PRIMARY GOAL ADDRESSED)	GOALS ADDRESSED	POTENTIAL OUTCOMES	MEASURES OF PROGRESS	NEXT STEPS	POTENTIAL PARTNERS	TIME FRAME
LAND USE						
Consider providing a density bonus for developments using a minimum percentage of deed restricted or managed affordable units.	• Land use	• Improve affordable housing opportunities	• Revised Development Code	• Research regional and national best practices • Establish a good percentage for Belmont • Revise the Land Development Code to include this incentive	Development community, builders	Year 1
Permit and encourage the development of accessory dwellings in single-family neighborhoods and establish design criteria to minimize their impact on adjacent properties and neighborhood character.	• Land use	• More affordable housing options • Greater opportunity for property owners to age in place	• Amendment of the Land Development Code	• Review zoning best practices related to accessory dwellings • Identify what criteria work best for Belmont • Update the Land Development Code	Neighborhood associations, builders	Year 1
Consider establishing a continuing care retirement community use as a by-right use in higher density residential and mixed-use districts.	• Land use	• More opportunities for local senior housing • Better accommodation of senior needs	• Amendment of the Land Development Code	• Review zoning best practices related to continuing care communities • Identify what criteria work best for Belmont • Update the Land Development Code	Senior community project developers, senior advocates	Year 1
Encourage mixed-residential subdivisions permitting a range of residential types as opposed to single-type subdivisions permitting only one housing type.	• Land use	• More walkability and active transportation options • More opportunity to preserve permanent open space • More opportunity to age within a given neighborhood	• Number of mixed-residential subdivisions	• Review the Land Development Code to determine how it should be amended to accommodate mixed-residential neighborhoods • Ensure that new standards encourage clustering and preservation of open space • Update the Land Development Code	Development community	Year 1
Ensure that the Land Development Code permits residential growth and development that allows residents to age in place within neighborhoods and small areas.	• Land use	• Greater opportunity for residents to age in their home or own their own lot in an accessory structure	• Amendment of the Land Development Code, if needed	• Review the Land Development Code to determine if it should be amended • If amendment is needed, research zoning best practices and development criteria that would be appropriate for Belmont • Update the Land Development Code, if needed	Development community	Year 1
Ensure that the policies and standards of the Land Development Code support and strengthen existing neighborhoods such as North Belmont and the Reid Neighborhood and areas for which a neighborhood conservation plan has been completed.	• Land use	• Stronger neighborhoods • Stabilized or improving property values	• # of variances needed • Property values over time	• Review the Land Development Code for its impacts on neighborhoods • Identify provisions that should be revised to minimize negative impacts and support and strengthen neighborhoods • Update the Land Development Code	Neighborhood associations	On going
Discourage residential development and uplifts, including significant increases in building mass, within existing residential areas that lead to or worsen the effects of gentrification.	• Land use • Community character	• Stronger existing and affordable housing neighborhoods	• Character of new housing compared to existing housing	• Review the Land Development Code and other policies that impact construction in existing residential neighborhoods to assess their impact on gentrification • Identify how the code and policies should be amended to better support existing building and lot patterns • Revise the code and policies, if needed	Neighborhood associations, builders, residents, property owners	Year 1
Improve the City's gateways by: • Encouraging the right mix of land uses and controls through changes in the Land Development Code and Zoning Map; • Using gateway signage and design to brand Belmont and set it apart from the region; and • Landscaping	• Land use • Community character	• Better entrances • Improved image • Stronger economic development position	• # gateway enhancement projects completed • Public opinion of gateways	• Assess the needs for each gateway • Create a plan for gateway enhancements • Update the Land Development Code and Zoning Map as needed • Prioritize gateways for improvement • Secure funding	Business owners, property owners, developers, local master gardeners and gardening groups, NCDOT	Short-term
Encourage appropriate adaptive re-use of older buildings.	• Land use	• Preserved historic buildings	• Older buildings successfully adapted for re-use	• Develop an inventory of existing vacant buildings • Identify potential appropriate uses for each building given its location and context within this plan • Market buildings for appropriate uses	Property owners, builders, realtors, Historic Preservation Commission	On-going
Ensure that adaptive reuse is not prevented or discouraged through unnecessary Land Development Code restrictions or building regulations.	• Land use • Community character	• Better use of existing buildings • Maintenance of community character	• Number of existing buildings that are vacant due to codes	• Develop an inventory of existing vacant buildings and identify which are important to Belmont • Talk to property owners to determine why they are vacant • If necessary, revise codes • If necessary, petition the county to adopt the existing building code	Property owners, Gaston County, Main Street Advisory Board	On-going

Our Town **Belmont**

VI. GETTING THERE **241**

This page from the *Our Town Belmont: Comprehensive Blueprint for Our Future* (2018) provides a good example of an implementation matrix that includes not only actions, the plan goals that they address, and potential outcomes, but also next steps and potential partners. Courtesy of the Town of Belmont.

- *Additional research and planning.* In some cases, subsequent investigation and planning may be appropriate. This may take the form of small-area plans (e.g., downtown master plan), functional plans (infrastructure plan or bicycle plan), or other targeted planning efforts.

Template 5A is an implementation toolbox, listing many categories and types of local government plan implementation.

The next task is to **select the most-appropriate strategies** for your community and prioritize them. You can review the list of tools set out above and identify which ones are most likely to be effective for your local government. To do this, you will need to ask which strategies (1) will advance the community's stated goals and (2) are feasible, given the community's resources, capacity, and expertise.

After selecting the tools to assist in choosing and prioritizing planning strategies/projects, it would be helpful to **summarize the recommended projects in an implementation table**. This table should list attributes such as the project name, the lead party responsible for implementing the project, the timeline, the cost, the relative priority of the project, and potential funding sources.

Other Potential Tasks

- Time and resources permitting, you can **conduct a more-detailed implementation feasibility assessment**. Many plans list dozens of potential implementation projects—a portfolio that far outstrips the community's available resources and capacity. Some of these measures are well aligned with community goals, while others may not be. A large number of projects can be overwhelming to local government staff responsible for implementation and can create false expectations on the part of stakeholders regarding what is going to happen in the community as a result of the planning effort. As a result, if time and resources allow, it might be helpful to conduct an implementation feasibility assessment to help ensure a thorough vetting of potential projects to yield an array of measures that staff and community stakeholders strongly believe can be successfully implemented.

Resources

The appendix contains an implementation toolbox (Template 5A) and a sample implementation checklist (Template 5B). For insight on how to develop an effective implementation component to a plan, look at the resources available from the American Planning Association (APA) and other sources. The APA's *Sustaining Places* guidance (as described in the organization's *PAS Reports* 567 and 578) provides excellent suggestions for plan components, content, and process.

Step 6: Draft and Adopt the Plan

Purpose

The sixth step in the process is to adopt the plan. This involves drafting the final plan document and taking it through the required board review-and-approval process. Along the way, the project team will make final revisions to the plan, as needed, so that the governing board will feel comfortable adopting it. One might expect adopting a plan to be the last step in the planning process, but a plan is not effective without the implementation actions to be taken in Step 7.

Timeline

Depending on the complexity of the plan and the variations in the local process used to review and adopt it, it can often take at least four to eight weeks (and sometimes longer) for the plan to be reviewed and adopted by the planning board and governing board.

Products

The goals of this step are (1) to draft a plan that serves the future vision the community has established in Steps 3 through 5 and (2) to achieve successful governing board adoption of the plan, including any revisions identified in the plan review and adoption process.

Key Considerations

- Providing regular updates to (and receiving regular input from) the planning board and the governing board as the process moves forward can help keep their members abreast of the planning effort, give them an opportunity to build ownership of the plan project, and minimize surprises when they receive the final document for review. In turn, particularly if the planning and governing boards can provide input and be involved throughout the process, this can make the plan-adoption step much smoother.
- Special work sessions and one-on-one or small-group meetings with the planning board and the governing board are sometimes needed to answer members' questions, evaluate plan language, and incorporate member input.

- The flexibility to hold an extra meeting or two to engage certain stakeholders or to work through some key issues can often be important in efforts to demonstrate that all stakeholders have had a voice in the process. This can sometimes make the difference in getting the plan to the point where the governing board feels comfortable adopting it.
- Presentations to appointed boards and to the governing board should focus on key policy issues included in the plan.
- Holding public open houses on the plan immediately prior to the meetings at which the plan will be presented to the reviewing and adopting boards can provide a more informal opportunity to answer stakeholder questions, minimize confusion about plan components, and improve the quality of the comments offered at the microphone during the more formal public hearing. Often, these open houses include poster displays staffed by local government personnel and consultants.
- One question that often comes up is whether to revise a draft plan between the time it goes to the planning board and the time it is reviewed by the governing board. This can add extra time and expense, so one approach is to draft a companion list of suggested revisions and have it included for review and decision by the governing board.
- Giving planning board and governing board members the opportunity to read the plan and get their questions answered in advance of plan adoption is a key task in the planning process. However, sometimes it can be hard to get all board members to read the plan ahead of the adoption stage, especially if it is a long document. Sometimes, creating clear opportunities and invitations for questions with timelines attached can help prevent the situation in which decision makers procrastinate and identify reasons for delaying a decision about the plan, especially if it includes some tough issues.
- Plans are living documents and should be revisited and updated to reflect changing needs and desires in the community.

Key Tasks

Create a draft plan document. Having outlined existing conditions, engaged with the community, established plan goals, drafted a future land use map, and identified implementation strategies, it is now time to put these parts together into a cohesive and readable plan. Sometimes communities or service providers have a standard document template that can be used for the draft plan. A sample plan outline, organized around the key substantive elements identified earlier in this guidebook (Natural Resources and Hazards, Community Resources and Assets, Community Development and Housing, Economic Development, Public Facilities and Infrastructure, and Future Development Patterns), is provided in Template 6A.

Incorporating graphics and photos, to the extent possible, will make the resulting product more engaging and fun to read. At the end of the day, the plan needs to clearly and succinctly present the community's vision. Operating with this principle in mind will ensure that the plan will serve as a valuable policy reference and touchstone for making community decisions on land use proposals, public investments, programming, and partnerships. And the better the plan looks, the more people will read it and the more effectively it can help to market the community's vision.

Present the plan to appointed and elected boards. G.S. Chapter 160D requires that local governments adopt land use plans and comprehensive plans using the legislative process required for zoning text amendments. This means that, at a minimum, the proposed plan must be reviewed by the planning board, which will provide comments and a recommendation before the proposed plan moves on to the governing board for a final decision. Plan documents can be numerous and substantial. Given this, a board may need several meetings to receive the necessary staff or consultant presentations and to discuss all plan components. The plan-adoption process also includes at least one public hearing before the governing board, although some planning boards will also hold public hearings before providing a recommendation to the governing board. Check your community's ordinances to confirm what procedures—if any—might be required beyond the statutory. To provide an opportunity for community stakeholders to ask questions and provide final input outside the bright lights of the regular meeting, local governments sometimes like to hold an open house immediately prior to the board meetings at which the plan is going to be presented. With this in mind, it is good to plan out the review-and-adoption

Planning board meeting in the Town of Carthage. Photo by Ben Hitchings.

process with local staff to make sure it matches community needs. Template 6B is a public hearing cheat sheet to assist with procedures and timelines.

Other Potential Tasks

- **Lay out the plan using a professional graphic designer.** If resources are available, it may be worthwhile to hire a professional graphic designer to lay out the final plan. This can help improve the readability of the plan and strengthen the positive impression it makes upon readers. As briefly discussed above, an attractive plan document that people want to open will be used more frequently and help to increase the extent to which it is implemented.

Resources

The appendix contains a plan outline (Template 6A) and a "cheat sheet" to help prepare for public hearings (Template 6B).

Step 7: Move to Action

Purpose

The seventh step in the process is to move effectively from planning to implementation. This is where many community efforts falter because of process fatigue, lack of resources, changing leadership, and/or competing priorities. However, with thoughtful preparation and sound project management, a community can move seamlessly from planning to implementing the updated community vision and making tangible improvements on the ground.

Timeline

The work of implementing a plan takes years and is driven ultimately by the complexity and time needed to carry out the action measures selected for implementation.

Products

The primary products of this phase are projects that have been successfully implemented. A valuable byproduct can be the development of a can-do attitude in the community and staff who are skilled in project management.

Key Considerations

- Finding a mix of small and large projects can be helpful in gaining some early successes and maintaining momentum until resources can be secured for higher-impact initiatives.
- Demonstrating the ability to advance the community vision through successful project implementation can be important, especially in an environment where there is skepticism about the competence and value of government.
- One common implementation project is a major update to the community's development ordinance to align the rules for new development with the updated community goals set out in the new plan. A smooth and expeditious ordinance update is important (1) to minimize issues arising during the period when the plan and the ordinance are significantly different and (2) to update the ordinance while there is still community agreement regarding the plan.

■ Developing strong partnerships with other community organizations can be important to achieving plan goals, especially in an environment where there are limited local government resources.

Key Tasks

Prepare for implementation during the planning process. Work carried out during the earlier steps in the planning process can set the stage for effective plan implementation. A strong public-engagement process can build support for the resulting plan and foster champions who will advocate for the resources needed to carry out plan-implementation projects. A focused strategy-identification effort can yield a manageable and well-targeted portfolio of implementation projects. Some plans include an extensive list of implementation measures and, in so doing, risk overwhelming staff who are responsible for follow-up. Some plans might place a disproportionate amount of the burden on staff, inadvertently cutting off public engagement with, ownership of, and responsibility for the plan. Other processes work to prioritize a handful of projects for implementation, providing a clear focus for

The Town of Chapel Hill held a special training session on project-management techniques for its planning staff. Photo by Ben Hitchings.

staff and board efforts on the heels of plan adoption. Under this approach, the town/county manager or top executive has clarity as to which projects to advance and can focus on organizing the implementation team and securing the necessary resources.

Launch key implementation projects. A crucial step in advancing the implementation process is assembling project teams and selecting a project manager to lead each initiative. The project managers could be local government staff members, board members, stakeholders, or any other appropriate community leaders. After these selections are made, project staff can prepare a project charter that summarizes the purpose of the undertaking, identifies the client and the organizational sponsor, clarifies roles and responsibilities, and describes the deliverables. The staff may also draft a project-scope-and-work plan with tasks and timelines to guide the work and see it through to completion. Template 7A offers an example action checklist and Template 7B is a sample project charter for implementation projects.

Match the local budget cycle. Local government work is driven by the governing unit's annual budget, which provides a clear plan for spending public money. Development and adoption of the budget occurs on an annual cycle. The budget process includes reporting accomplishments from the past year, assessing needs, developing priorities for the coming year, projecting revenues and expenses, adopting the budget, and implementing the work plan. Synchronizing plan-implementation projects with the budget cycle to make sure that the necessary staff and resources are available when needed is essential to advancing the community's shared vision.

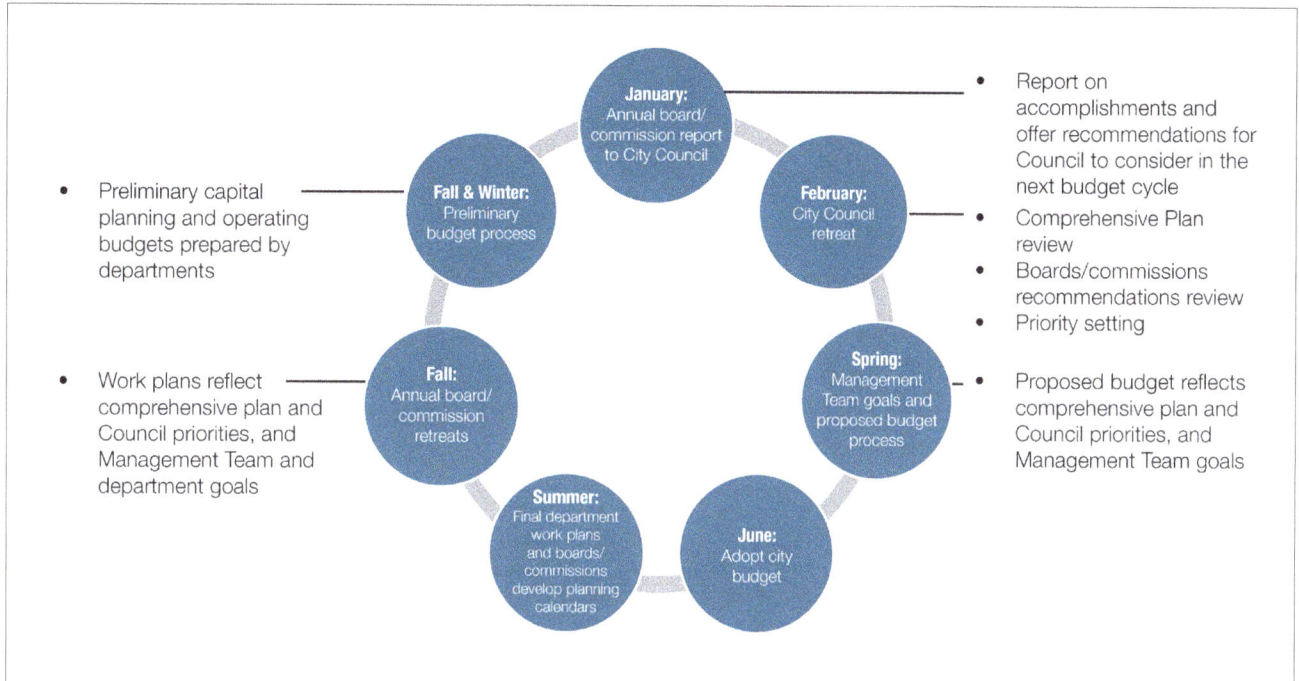

Graphic from the *Living Asheville Comprehensive Plan* (2018), 387, showing how to synchronize plan implementation projects with the annual budget cycle. Courtesy of the City of Asheville.

Other Potential Tasks

- **Conduct portfolio management.** Depending on the number of plan-implementation projects, it may be necessary to do some portfolio management to make strategic decisions about when to move different projects forward and how to distribute limited resources.
- **Provide an annual update.** It is very helpful to provide an annual report on plan progress to appointed and elected boards to motivate further progress and make course corrections as needed on the various plan-implementation projects.
- **Train staff and utilize project-management techniques.** It is often useful to train staff in project-management techniques to help them oversee projects more effectively. Frequently, smaller communities outsource project management to consultants, but they still need staff in-house to manage the project from the local government side.

Implementation Action	Timeline	Entity Responsible	Status - 2014	Status - 2012
Top Priority Implementation Actions				
1. Work with Wilson County to establish a tiered growth system	Initiate within one year	Planning and Development Services, Fire/Rescue Services, Police, Public Service, and Wilson Energy	We continue to use the tiered growth concept as a policy guide to inform decision making. As it was in 2012, development pressure on the edge of the City continues to be low.	As City policy, we use this idea of tiered growth in discussions with prospective developers. However, there is not a formal policy/system. The development pressure has been low and so this has not become a high priority item.
2. Amend Wilson's Land Development Ordinances	Initiate within one year	Planning and Development Services, with TRC Departments	The new development regulations were adopted January 2013. We are preparing to do a comprehensive review of the new code to gauge its effectiveness since its adoption.	In progress. As of March 2012, approximately 75% completed, with adoption expected late Summer.
3. Establish a neighborhood planning and implementation process	Initiate within two years	Planning and Development Services, Human Relations Office, Police Department	The Choice Neighborhood Plan was adopted by Council June 2014. The plan is presently with HUD for their final review and sign off. Implementation work is ongoing for both the Barton Area Plan and now the Choice Neighborhood Plan. One unfortunate setback in implementing the Barton Area Plan was the failure of the Landmark Project to secure tax credit financing for the Old Wilson project.	The first neighborhood plan was completed and adopted by City Council on March 15, 2012. The City is partnering with the Housing Authority to implement the Choice Neighborhood Initiative Planning Grant, which will create a neighborhood plan for the area between the railroad tracks and Highway 301.
4. Support and facilitate center city catalyst projects such as the Villages of Center City	Initiate within one year	Planning and Development Services, Community Development, Downtown Development Corporation, Public Services	Center City revitalization continues to be a focus of the City. Work is ongoing to kick start the Freeman Place project, our brownfield program continues to grow with a new $1,000,000 grant, and downtown revitalization has seen several successful projects completed in the last 2 years.	This is being implemented through partnership with the Housing Authority on the Choice Neighborhoods Initiative Grant (received 2012). Another way we are implementing this is through the Whirligig Park project downtown. Finally, the Brownfields Program seeks to incent redevelopment at abandoned or underused commercial/industrial sites in the center city.

Progress report on implementation of Wilson's 2030 comprehensive plan. Reprinted with permission from City of Wilson, *2030 Comprehensive Plan Progress Report* (2019), 1.

Resources

The appendix contains a sample project charter (Template 7A).

Clark, Terry A. *Project Management for Planners: A Practical Guide*. Chicago: American Planning Association, 2002.

Mendes, Diana C. *Project Management Is Good Planning!* PAS Memo September/October 2011. Chicago: American Planning Association, 2011.

Photo by Ben Hitchings.

Conclusion

This concludes our seven-step process for preparing a streamlined community land use plan or comprehensive plan and for doing it in a way that is both meaningful and fast. Below are a few closing thoughts to keep in mind as you prepare to take on this process.

- Be respectful at all times and make sure to show stakeholders that you're listening.
- Use public input and professional expertise to develop a plan that the community can successfully implement and that will advance its chosen goals.
- All too often, we find ourselves working in an environment where resources are limited. As a result, it is important to identify your community's highest-priority items and to focus on those when preparing the community plan. Also, take note that in crafting the plan you should strive for high quality but should never let the perfect be the enemy of the good, as they say. Your community can always update the plan to improve it in the future.
- Don't forget to have fun. Acting with this thought in mind will help engage stakeholders in the planning process and will build a positive environment for envisioning the future of the community.

By following this process, both planning service providers and communities can meet the requirements of G.S. Chapter 160D and deliver a plan document that can shape the community in positive ways for years to come.

Worksheets and Templates

Template 1A. Sample Project Timeline

PlanNC Playbook
Worksheet #0: Sample Project Timeline
UNC School of Government
(Draft, 4-20-21)

TASKS	MONTH 1			MONTH 2			MONTH 3			MONTH 4			MONTH 5			MONTH 6			MONTH 7			MONTH 8			MONTH 9			MONTH 10		
	1	2	3	4	5	6	7	8	9	##	11	12	13	14	15	16	17	18	19	20	21	22	23	24	25	26	27	28	29	30	31	32	33	34	35	36	37	38	39	40	41	42	43
Step 1: Summarize Existing Conditions																																										
1.1 Gather and present available community data																																										
1.2 Review existing community plans																																										
1.3 Interview key stakeholders																																										
1.4 Conduct site tour																																										
1.5 Other potential tasks?																																										
Step 2: Engage the Community																																										
2.1 Create website links																																										
2.2 Hold community workshop																																										
2.3 Hold open houses																																										
2.4 Conduct public hearings																																										
2.5 Other potential tasks?																																										
Step 3: Set Goals and Policies																																										
3.1 Synthesize public input																																										
3.2 Draft goals and policies																																										
3.3 Other potential tasks?																																										
Step 4: Map the Future																																										
4.1 Conduct change analysis																																										
4.2 Create a Future Land Use Map (FLUM)																																										
4.3 Other potential tasks?																																										
Step 5: Identify Implementation Strategies																																										
5.1 Identify potential implementation strategies																																										
5.2 Select appropriate implementation strategies																																										
5.3 Create a summary table																																										
5.4 Other potential tasks?																																										
Step 6: Adopt the Plan																																										
6.1 Draft plan document																																										
6.2 Present plan to appointed and elected boards																																										
6.3 Other potential tasks?																																										
Step 7: Move to Action																																										
7.1 Prepare for implementation during planning process																																										
7.2 Launch key implementation projects																																										
7.3 Match local budget cycle																																										
7.4 Other potential tasks?																																										

NOTES:
1. Modify this table as desired.
2. Consider adding subtasks that outline how to complete each key task.
3. Consider highlighting key project milestones.
4. Consider identifying ongoing management tasks and key client check-in points.

Template 1B. Existing Conditions Data Worksheet

This worksheet provides a checklist and template for gathering and analyzing data to build out the existing conditions of a community. The worksheet includes general data topics, key variables to check off, a space for analyzing data, and a section to highlight key takeaways.

Demographics		Community	County	State
Total population	Year			
	10 years prior			
Median age				
Population under 18 years (%)				
Population 65 years and over (%)				
Race (%)	White			
	Black			
	Asian			
	Native American			
	Other			
Ethnicity (%)	Latino			
	Non-Latino			
Median household income				
No. (%) in poverty				
Persons with disability (%)				
Persons under age 65 without health insurance (%)				
High-school graduate or higher (age 25+)				
Bachelor's degree or higher (age 25+)				
Households with computer (%)				
Households with broadband internet subscription (%)				

Demographics, *continued*

		Community	County	State
Other data (examples: household type, disability)				
Key takeaways				
Clarifying questions	1. How is the community's population changing over time (growing, declining, or staying the same)? 2. What are the population characteristics of the community (e.g. % ethnic minorities compared with county and state, % people in poverty compared with county and state, etc.)? 3. Summarize the demographic characteristics and the issues that need to be considered (poverty, aging, digital inclusion, etc.).			
Notes:				

Land Use and Development

Land area (in square miles)	

Land Use and Development, *continued*	
Population per square mile	
Existing land use (% of land area in different land use categories—customize)	
Planned future land use (% of land area in different land use categories—customize)	
Current zoning districts (% of land area in different zoning categories—customize)	
Number and type of rezoning cases by year in recent years	
Number, value, and type of building permits issued by year in recent years	

Land Use and Development, *continued*

Other data (examples: land use polices, other land use or conservation plans)	
Key takeaways	
Clarifying questions	1. What are the current land use patterns? 2. Is planned future land use consistent with zoning? What are the reasons for the inconsistencies? Does zoning or land use plan need to be adjusted or modified? 3. Does the planned future land use support the goals and future development needs of the small town (for housing, education, infrastructure, historic preservation, etc.)? 4. How many different plans are in place that affect the municipality? 5. What specific locations are designated for signficant change (redevelopment, demolishment, zoning, etc.)?

Notes:

Economics and Employment

	Community	County	State
Percent in civilian labor force (age 16+)			
Percent female in civilian labor force (age 16+)			
Total workforce population			
Total no. of businesses			
Man-owned firms			

Economics and Employment, *continued*			
	Community	**County**	**State**
Woman-owned firms			
Minority-owned firms			
Nonminority-owned firms			
Total retail sales			
Total retail sales per capita			
Main industries and occupations (list below)			
Other data			
Key takeaways			
Clarifying questions	1. What are the town's goals for economic development? Does the town want to see growth? 2. How is employment changing over time? How does current employment compare to that in 2007, before the last recession? 3. How slow or fast has employment growth been after the last recession?		
Notes:			

Housing			
	Community	**County**	**State**
Households			
Total housing units			
Average household size			
Vacant units (%)			
Owner-occupied-housing-unit rate			
No. and % of Owners			
Average year housing built			
Median gross rent			
Median home value			
No. of units in structure			
Cost-burdened households (%)			
Other data			
Key takeaways			
Clarifying questions	1. How do owner-occupied rates compare with county and state averages? 2. What portion of renters are cost-burdened (more than 30% of income paid toward housing costs)? How does this reflect trends identified during economic analysis? 3. What are the biggest challenges associated with housing in your community (e.g., aging housing stock, lack of affordable options, lack of apartments vs. single-family homes or vice versa)?		
Notes:			

Transportation and Infrastructure	
Means of transportation (mode split; select categories)	
Mean travel time to work (workers age 16+)	
Persons who work outside community	
Persons who live and work in community	
Persons who commute into community for work	
Annual average daily traffic (select roadways)	
Location of employment centers and residential areas	
Location and numbers of public services (education, health care, etc.)	
Location and number lowest-income households and zero-car households	
Other data	
Key takeaways	

Transportation and Infrastructure, *continued*	
Clarifying questions	1. What does the commuting pattern look like? Where are the employment centers and where are the residential areas? How long do workers need to travel to their workplace? What's their travel mode? Where are the zero-car households and lowest-income households? Is there demand or support for transportation modes other than driving (like walking, biking, or transit)? 2. Where are the current facilities for walking, biking, and transit? Are there any safety concerns? (Need data from local government.) 3. Where are the households that don't have access to heating equipment (or rely on unsustainable heating sources)? Where are the local public services (schools, sewerage, medical facilities, etc.)? Where are the residents who don't have access to those services?
Notes:	

Environment		
Locations of the 100-year and 500-year flood zones (floodplain data from FEMA)		
Terrain conditions (the slope distribution across the town)		
Whether the community faces landslide issues and locations of any such issues		
Land-use / land-cover data (customize categories of developed land / impervious surfaces vs. fields vs. forests)		
Water bodies and their classifications		
Air Quality Index report	Conditions of air quality for the town in the past	
	Pollutant has commonly been seen in the past (if any)	
Air Quality Statistics report	Whether the air quality of the town met the EPA standards in the past	
Monitor Values Report (if any major pollutants)	The level of the major pollutants for the town	
Other data		
Key takeaways		

Environment, *continued*	
Clarifying questions	1. What areas are more or less suitable for future development considering all the environmental resources and risks? 2. Are any current developed areas facing risks from flooding, landslides, air pollution, or other natural hazards? 3. For communities with expected growth, to what extent can the existing land supply support additional people and jobs?
Notes:	

Other Community Plans	
Transportation plans (link and name)	
Hazard-mitigation plans: (link and name)	
Other plans (parks and recreation, housing, economic development)	
Key takeaways	
Clarifying questions	1. How many different plans are in place that affect the municipality? 2. What specific locations are designated for large change (redevelopment, demolishment, zoning, etc.)? 3. Which policies in the various plans are consistent? 4. Which policies in the various plans conflict?
Notes:	

Building a community narrative

Next steps

Questions to verify through community engagement

Template 2A. Community Engagement Plan

Community engagement is a process of involving and empowering community members and organizations to inform the planning process. This worksheet can help you gather the necessary information to develop a customized community engagement strategy for the community planning process.

Part 1: Identifying the Key Elements and Players

Sit down with local planning officials and work through the following questions together.

1. Identify Goals
   a. What are your goals for community engagement? (Think beyond compliance with 160D.)

   _____
   _____
   _____
   _____
   _____

   b. What parts of your comprehensive plan do you want to receive community input on?

   ☐ Housing
   ☐ General visioning & values
   ☐ Regional connection

   ☐ Recreation
   ☐ Health & wellness
   ☐ Historical preservation

   ☐ Transportation
   ☐ Land use
   ☐ Other: _____

2. Identify Stakeholders

   A stakeholder is a person or group who has an interest or concern in something, or who will be impacted by the decision or plan. Examples include business owners, community groups, local organizations, churches, schools, families with children, retirees, other residents, elected officials, local staff, etc.

   a. Who are the key groups that will be affected by a new comprehensive plan for your community? Identify at least one key community leader or member from each group who could help organize the community engagement process. Think outside the box!

Comprehesive Plan's Stakeholders		
Group	**Unique Contributions It Can Make**	**Key Contact**
Ex: business owners	*speak to the needs and desires of the commercial sector*	*John Doe* *john@doe.org*

    b. Which groups listed above are not usually involved or are underrepresented in local decisions? Are there any groups missing?

_____

_____

_____

3. Identify Resources

    a. Do you have a budget for community engagement? _____

    b. Which local staff and volunteers could help with community engagement? *Examples: staffing events, presenting to community groups, performing administrative tasks.*

Staff and Volunteers for Community Engagement		
Staff/volunteer name	**Time to contribute (hours/week)**	**Role**

4. Identify Existing Opportunities

    a. What are some community hubs and events where people congregate? For each event, include the date. *Examples: parades, festivals, farmers markets, schools, libraries, churches, popular downtown businesses, post offices.*

_____

_____

_____

    b. What communication resources do you currently use to engage or inform your residents? *Examples: listservs, newsletters, a local website, social media, a newspaper.*

_____

_____

_____

    c. What other communication resources might be helpful?

_____

_____

_____

5. Identify Challenges & Limitations

    a. Have you undertaken a community engagement process in the past? What made it successful or challenging? *Examples: public works projects, grant applications.*

_____

_____

_____

b. What constituencies are most likely to participate? Are there others that might be less able or willing to participate?

_____

_____

_____

c. What concerns might people have about getting involved? What barriers might they face?

_____

_____

_____

d. How can these barriers be overcome?

_____

_____

_____

e. Are there any sensitive subjects, taboos, or controversial topics in the community that may need special treatment or consideration?

_____

_____

_____

f. How could more community engagement be encouraged or incentivized?

_____

_____

_____

Part 2: Opportunities and Limitations

Based on the information gathered in your interview with local planning staff, list some of the opportunities and limitations for engagement in this community in the table below.

Opportunities and Limitations for Community Engagement	
Opportunities	Limitations

Part 3: Engagement Techniques

The table below lists a number of different techniques that might be employed to obtain additional public input. Consider which of the methods below might be best for the community with which you are working.

Methods of Engaging the Community			
Method	**Benefit(s)**	**Cost ($–$$$)**	**Time commitment**
Public meetings	Reaches large numbers of residents	$$–$$$	High
Open house	Flexible space for informing and gathering input	$$–$$$	High
Community workshop	Structured space for topic-specific community brainstorming	$$–$$$	High
Stakeholder interviews	Reaches key community representatives; flexible location	$$	Moderate
Focus groups	Facilitates conversation and exchange between community stakeholders	$$	Moderate
Surveys	Wide reach; doesn't require attendance; quantitative data	$$$	Moderate
Paper/mail	Accessibility for those without Internet; older generations; doesn't require tech resources	$$-$$$	High
Digital	Younger generations; faster response time	$$	Moderate
Online engagement	Wide reach; no time, location, or cost restraints for residents	$-$$	Flexible
Social media	Ability to bring community engagement into everyday life; sharing of recorded content; ease of dissemination	$	Low
Website	Central location; can hold multiple forms of engagement	$$	Moderate
Email listservs	Direct communication prevents misinformation	$	Low
Tabling	Integration into important existing community hubs and events	$$	Moderate

Given the identified opportunities and challenges, and using the reference table above, what community engagement techniques would be most feasible and effective for this community?

_____

_____

_____

_____

_____

_____

Template 2B. Sample Interview Questions for Town Staff

These questions are designed for the service provider to ask at the outset of the project to help understand existing conditions and key issues. They are intended to support a thirty-to-sixty-minute interview with each key staff person.

Planning Process and Engagement

1. What would make the planning process a success?
   a. What would you like to avoid in the planning process?
2. What are the current political dynamics in the community?
   a. Who are the leaders of the community?
   b. Are there political or other interest groups that play a large role in local politics?
3. Who are the key stakeholders whom we should plan to interview for the planning process?
4. How active are stakeholders in the community? What are the best ways to engage the community?
   a. List two to three major stakeholder groups or individuals.

Baseline Data

5. What features (such as neighborhoods, natural resources, commercial areas, employers, etc.) help to define your community and make it special?
6. What are the key natural resources for your community? In what ways has your community been affected by natural hazards?
7. Has the community conducted planning projects in the past? If so,
   a. What worked well, and what were the lessons learned?
   b. How successful has the community been in implementing its plans?
   c. Can you provide a copy of that plan?
8. What baseline information can you provide relating to public facilities and infrastructure? This might include reports, maps, data, or other information.

Community Priorities

9. Are there any things the planning team should know as it starts this project?
   a. Things to celebrate and support?
   b. Things to watch out for?
   c. Things to avoid?
10. What are the main issues that you would like to see addressed through the planning process?
    a. What challenges and opportunities keep you up at night?
11. What other information would you like to share about your community or the planning process?

Template 2C. Interview Questions for Key Stakeholders

These questions are designed for the service provider to ask at the outset of the project to help understand existing conditions and key issues. They are intended to support a thirty-to-sixty-minute interview with each key stakeholder.

Opening Interview Statement

Consider opening the interview by saying that you would like the interviewee's help in learning about some of the key issues and considerations at the outset of the planning process.

Questions

1. What are the main issues that you would like to see addressed through the planning process? What challenges and opportunities keep you up at night?

2. What features help to define your community and make it special?

3. What features in the community would you like to see protected?

4. What features would you like to see added to the community?

5. Identify examples of new development that you would like to see in the years ahead.

6. Identify examples of new development that you would like to avoid in the years ahead.

7. What would make this planning process a success?

8. What other information would you like to share about your community or the planning process?

If interviewees have trouble answering questions 2, 3, or 4, consider asking about features in the following categories:

- Natural Resources and Hazards (e.g., farmland, flooding);
- Community Resources and Assets (e.g., parks and recreation facilities, beautiful views)
- Community Development and Housing (e.g., range of housing types, areas of need);
- Economic Development (e.g., trends, assets, and opportunities);
- Public Facilities and Infrastructure (e.g., transportation needs, funding sources); or
- Future Development Patterns (e.g., preferred development types, locational considerations).

Template 2D. Sample Community Workshop Agenda

This community workshop is intended to provide a key component in the public-engagement process for the plan. This is one of many ways that it could be structured.

Advance Activities

In the weeks leading up to the workshop, advertise the event broadly and try to build interest and excitement about it. Enlist volunteers to help get the word out.

Supplies

Potential supplies to bring include audio-visual equipment, tables, seating, flip charts, easels, sticky notes, thick pens with assorted colors, sign-in sheets, handouts, and food.

Immediately before Starting the Meeting

Set up a fun self-serve exercise as participants come into the meeting room (or join the meeting virtually). One example would be to display a map of the community and ask participants to identify their favorite places or the places where they go the most.

Meeting Agenda

1. Welcome (Mayor, Planning Board Chair, or Town Manager)

2. Introduction to the Project (Town Manager, Planning Director, or Planning Consultant)
   a. Give a presentation describing why we're here and what the purpose of the project is.
   b. Provide a general outline of the schedule.
   c. Highlight opportunities for public involvement.

3. "Snow Cards" Sticky-Note Exercise (Planning Consultant)
   a. Distribute thick pens with dark colors and large sticky notes (extra sticky).
   b. Ask workshop participants a series of questions, such as the following:
      - What makes our community special?
      - What features would you most like to see preserved in the community?
      - What features would you most like to see added to the community?

4. Small-Group Breakout Discussions
   a. Prior to the meeting, identify three to six key topics. Consider using the following:
      - Natural Resources and Hazards (e.g., farmland, flooding)
      - Community Resources and Assets (e.g., parks and recreation facilities, beautiful views)
      - Community Development and Housing (e.g., range of housing types, areas of need)
      - Economic Development (e.g., trends, assets, and opportunities)
      - Public Facilities and Infrastructure (e.g., transportation needs, funding sources)
      - Future Development Patterns (e.g., preferred development types, locational considerations)
   b. Resources permitting, gather key information and statistics about these issues.
   c. At the beginning of the meeting, display the topics you identified on posters set on easels to create a station with chairs on each topic.
   d. Designate a staff or consultant facilitator to conduct a small-group discussion at each station, asking two or three questions.

    e. Capture comments on flip charts.

    f. Rotate workshop participants through all the stations.

    g. Consider something fun like stamping tickets at each station and then entering each ticket with a complete set of stamps into a drawing for prizes donated by local businesses.

5. Conclude the Meeting

    a. Thank the participants, and describe the next steps in the planning process.

Template 2E. Governing Board Progress Report

A comprehensive plan represents a shared community vision that can affect land use and development in a given community for years to come. As a result, the elected officials on your governing board—not to mention members of the public who have provided input—may be keenly interested in the progress of the planning process. Providing periodic updates will keep the plan-development process transparent and meet this need for information.

In addition, stakeholders might approach board members to inquire about the status of the planning process. Board members should be updated regularly on where the process stands so that they can respond knowledgeably if this kind of question arises.

Below are sample templates for an update presentation to the governing board at one of its regular meetings and a short-form staff report.

In-Meeting Verbal Update

The template below can be used as a script for presenting a progress update to the governing board.

Good evening, [*members of the governing board*].

As you may recall, North Carolina General Statutes now require that all local governments that wish to enforce zoning regulations must have a reasonably maintained comprehensive plan or land use plan by July 1, 2022. The [*town/city/county*] has undertaken this planning process not only to comply with this requirement but also to develop a shared vision for the future use of land and for investments in infrastructure and other community systems to support that vision, along with a map and action plan for how to get there.

[*Today/Tonight*] we will update you on where this planning process stands and where it is going.

The process of developing a new [*comprehensive / land use*] plan for the community started when [*the governing board authorized this process / staff initiated this process*] in [*Month*] 2021.

[*Review at a high level your overall timeline and process for development and approval of the plan. The seven steps used in this guide represent an example of one way to organize the timing, trajectory, and milestones of the project.*]

At this point, [*Identify the currently active step of the process.*]

Most recently, [*Describe events since the last governing board meeting, including public meetings, staff reviews, presentations to the governing board, etc.*]

Next, we are scheduled to hold [*describe additional events or other next steps*] and to [*take other actions—develop a draft plan for the governing or planning board, etc.*]

Once that [*occurs / is complete*], we will be able to move to [*following step in the process*], and we hope to have a draft plan ready for your review on [*date.*]

Up to this point, we have been hearing and finding [*Identify two to three themes emerging from recent events and research.*]

Finally, in the interest of creating a shared vision that can be supported by a wide cross-section of the community, we have connected with a number of key stakeholders, neighborhoods, and constituencies, including [*Identify key constituencies, particularly underserved or underrepresented groups and stakeholders.*] We also hope to reach [*Identify some other target constituencies for next steps, unless the public-engagement process is complete.*]

Staff Report

Staff presentations are often accompanied by a written report. If you provide such a report when giving progress updates on your plan process, the text below can be used as a template for that staff report.

North Carolina General Statutes now require that all local governments that wish to enforce zoning regulations must have a reasonably maintained comprehensive plan or land use plan by July 1, 2022. The [*town/city/county*] has undertaken this planning process not only to comply with this requirement but also to develop a shared vision for the future use of land and for investments in infrastructure and other community systems to support that vision, along with a map and action plan for how to get there.

The process of developing a new [*comprehensive / land use*] plan for the community started when [*the governing board authorized this process / staff initiated this process*] in [*Month*] 2021.

[*Review at a high level your overall timeline and process for development and approval of the plan. The seven steps used in this guide represent an example of one way to organize the timing, trajectory, and milestones of the project.*]

Current step: [*Identify the currently active step of the process.*]

Most-recent completed actions: [*Describe events and actions since the last governing board meeting, including public meetings, staff reviews, presentations to the governing board, etc.*]

Upcoming actions: [*List two to three upcoming events or actions, like holding a plan open house in a key neighborhood, developing a draft plan for the governing or planning board, etc.*]

Emerging themes: [*Identify two to three themes emerging from recent events and research.*]

In the interest of creating a shared vision that can be supported by a wide cross-section of the community, we have connected with a number of key stakeholders, neighborhoods, and constituencies, including [*Identify key constituencies, particularly underserved or underrepresented groups and stakeholders.*]

We also hope to reach [*Identify some other target constituencies for next steps, unless the public-engagement process is complete.*]

Template 3A. Public Engagement Synthesis Worksheet

Public participation in the planning process can come in a variety of forms. Input returned from public outreach efforts can touch on issues across the spectrum of a community's challenges and opportunities, suggest a range of potential action items, and provide different perspectives on the direction the community should take in the future. This worksheet is designed to help take the information collected from these efforts and condense it into actionable themes that can guide the remaining steps of the planning process.

Live Sessions

Participation

List the types of meetings, open houses, town halls, or other events that you held to gather public input.

_____
_____
_____

What stakeholder groups or constituencies were represented at these sessions? Was an effort made to reach out to certain hard-to-reach constituencies?

_____
_____
_____

Were there any constituencies that you tried to reach that were not heard from? If so, did they participate in other public engagement offerings or are there other ways you could seek input from these constituencies?

_____
_____
_____

Themes and Takeaways

Review the comments you received from each of the above events. Based on those comments, identify three to five key comments regarding Natural Resources and Hazards. Key comments would be comments that you heard multiple times, areas of agreement across constituencies, or particularly unique aspects of the natural area within and around the community.

_____
_____
_____

Now identify three to five key comments regarding Community Resources and Assets.

_____
_____
_____

Identify three to five key comments regarding Community Development and Housing. For example, is there a need to address substandard housing? Is there a need for more affordable housing?

_____

_____

_____

Identify three to five key comments regarding Economic Development. These can relate to the community's current economic state, to physical or market spaces that the community could enter, or to where it could expand its reach.

_____

_____

_____

Identify three to five key comments regarding Public Facilities and Infrastructure.

_____

_____

_____

Identify three to five key comments regarding Future Development Patterns and the future growth of the community.

_____

_____

_____

Asynchronous Public Engagement (Outside of Public Engagement Events)

Participation

Did you receive comments via phone, email, website submission, or hard copy (drop box or mailbox)? If so, which of these methods did you use?

_____

_____

_____

What stakeholders or constituencies participated via phone, email, web, or hard copy? Are these similar constituencies to those who participated in live sessions, or did you reach different groups of people?

_____

_____

_____

Review the sets of stakeholders and constituencies that submitted comments. Then review the list of stakeholders and constituencies that participated in public outreach events. What sectors of your community were not represented, and how might you reach them?

_____

_____

_____

Themes and Takeaways

Review the comments you received from each of the above asynchronous opportunities for input. Based on those comments, identify three to five key comments regarding Natural Resources and Hazards.

_____

_____

_____

Now identify three to five key comments regarding Community Resources and Assets.

_____

_____

_____

Identify three to five key comments regarding Community Development and Housing. For example, is there a need to address substandard housing? Is there a need for more affordable housing?

_____

_____

_____

Identify three to five key comments regarding Economic Development. These can relate to the community's current economic state, to physical or market spaces that the community could enter, or to where it could expand its reach.

_____

_____

_____

Identify three to five key comments regarding Public Facilities and Infrastructure.

_____

_____

_____

Identify three to five key comments regarding Future Development Patterns and the future growth of the community.

_____

_____

_____

Template 3B. Developing Goals Worksheet

This worksheet is designed to turn the themes identified in the public engagement synthesis worksheet (Template 3A) into a set of goals that can be further refined in later steps of the planning process and can inform the direction of the comprehensive or land use plan. You may find that you enter similar (or even the same) ideas or inputs in different parts of the worksheet. This is perfectly fine; it suggests that the repeat responses are important plan inputs!

Part 1: Existing Conditions

Look back at your findings from "Step 1: Summarize Existing Conditions." Use the results of that process to answer the following questions:

1. Were any natural hazards or constraints identified in your summary of existing conditions? If so, what were they?

2. Are there environmental, scenic, or cultural resources that add to the community's identity or economy? What might be done to protect or enhance these resources?

3. What does your data say about demographic growth and change in the community?

4. What do these results say about the community's economic development? What opportunities are there for additional economic growth and development?

5. What investments in infrastructure and facilities might be suggested by the demographic growth (or lack thereof) identified in the data?

Part 2: Community Input

Review your public engagement synthesis worksheet from "Step 3: Set Goals and Policies." Divide the key comments you identified into opportunities and challenges for each of the six elements described in the introduction to this guidebook:

Natural Resources and Hazards

Opportunities: _____

Challenges: _____

Community Resources and Assets

Opportunities: _____

Challenges: _____

Community Development and Housing

Opportunities: _____

Challenges: _____

Economic Development

Opportunities: _____

Challenges: _____

Public Facilities and Infrastructure

Opportunities: _____

Challenges: _____

Future Development Patterns

Opportunities: _____

Challenges: _____

Describe the broader community vision expressed in the public-engagement process. What characteristics has the public suggested that it wants its community to have?

_____

Part 3: Staff Input

Now consider your own experiences in this community. What additional challenges and opportunities does the community face that might not be reflected in public comments?

_____

_____

_____

Part 4: Accentuating Positives, Eliminating Negatives

Your responses to the questions below, based on your responses to the questions in Parts 1, 2, and 3, can provide the starting point for a list of proposed goals. You can also reference the implementation toolbox (Template 5A) for ideas.

1. What are some ways in which the community could take advantage of its natural resources?

   _____

2. What are some ways in which the community could manage its environmental challenges?

   _____

3. What are some ways in which the community could preserve its assets and leverage its resources?

   _____

4. What are some ways in which the community could take advantage of its housing and community development assets?

   _____

5. What are some ways in which the community could meet the challenges identified regarding housing and community development?

   _____

6. What are some ways in which the community could leverage its advantages (if any) related to public facilities and infrastructure?

   _____

7. What are some ways in which the community could meet the identified challenges related to public facilities and infrastructure?

   _____

8. Does the community face the demands of a high growth or a need to encourage more growth?

   _____

9. What are some ways in which the community could encourage desired future development growth patterns?

   _____

10. How else can the community respond to the key takeaways from the public-engagement process?

_____

Part 5: Putting It All Together

Look at your responses to the other questions in this part of the worksheet. Draft a list of five to ten goals that the community might pursue, based on those responses.

_____
_____
_____
_____
_____

Template 4A. Mapping Checklist: Creating a Future Land Use Map

This worksheet is designed to help you conduct a "change analysis" of your community, identify current and future place types in the community, and prepare a future land use map (FLUM). Start by identifying what areas should be preserved, what areas should be enhanced, what areas should be transitioned, and what areas should be transformed over the next ten to twenty years.

Step 1

Take a map of the community and draw blobs around the areas that should be preserved, enhanced, transitioned, or transformed. As you do this, work to align these choices to synchronize with and advance the community vision expressed in the planning process. For example, the community might want to preserve important natural areas, enhance existing neighborhoods, transition selected resource lands to new housing development, and transform an aging commercial area.

Step 2

Describe the different places in the community today. The following are some example place types:

Green Spaces

- Park
- Greenway
- Natural area
- Resource land (e.g., a farmland or a forestland)

Residential Neighborhoods

- Urban
- Multi-family
- Small-lot
- Suburban
- Semi-rural
- Rural living

Commercial Districts

- Main street commercial
- Regional commercial
- Suburban commercial
- Neighborhood commercial
- Rural crossroads
- Mixed-use center
- Mixed-use neighborhood

Institutional Districts

- Employment campus
- Educational campus
- Medical campus
- Civic and institutional
- Worship

Industrial Development

- Light industrial/warehouse
- Heavy industrial
- Airport

Step 3

Identify and map the places that the community would like to have in the future, drawing from the list above and other resources, retaining the places that should be preserved and enhanced, and changing the places that should be transitioned and transformed. As you do this, check to make sure these land use assignments synchronize with the community vision expressed in the planning process. The resulting product will be a draft of the FLUM.

Examples

- If a community wants to redevelop an old factory into shops and housing, this property might go from light industrial to mixed-use center in the FLUM.
- If the community wants to strengthen its main street and connect it to a community park through a dilapidated residential area, the existing land between the main street and the park might go from small-lot neighborhood to main street commercial in the FLUM.
- If a community wants to add more infill housing, certain properties might go from vacant to one of the residential categories in the FLUM.
- If a community wants to add more greenfield housing, land might go from resource lands to suburban neighborhood in the FLUM.

Step 4

Once you have a draft of the FLUM, you can then share this with community stakeholders and decision makers, at a community workshop or online for example, to get feedback and make refinements.

Template 5A. Implementation Toolbox

A plan is only as good as its implementation. This implementation toolbox is intended as a quick guide to help North Carolina local governments as they take actions to further the goals identified in the planning process. This toolbox is intended as a simplified list of common implementation actions; it is by no means an exhaustive list. There are certainly more options than those listed here.

Considerations and Uses

The list below of implementation actions is organized into distinct categories, ranging from local rules and funding priorities to partnerships and public outreach and more.

The list may be used at the start of the planning process to focus discussions on topics that are within the scope of the local government's authority. It may also be used in crafting the implementation action items for the community plan. Finally, the list may be used to review and evaluate whether a near-final plan includes the full range of implementation options.

This toolbox is framed with open-ended phrasing because one type of action may be appropriate for many different goals. For example, a town may want to prioritize several different topics in its staff annual work plan and may also want to partner with the county on several different implementation actions. Additionally, one goal may be served by action from several different implementation categories. So, for example, if a town's stated goal is "Promote infill development," the implementation actions might include actions from throughout the toolbox: updated town regulations, investment in improved utility capacity, partnerships with existing neighborhood associations, a small-area plan, and more.

Implementation Toolbox

Local Policies, Regulations, and Jurisdiction

- Review and amend zoning, subdivision, or other development regulations to _____.
- Rezone _____ (specific area) to align with _____.
- Enhance and enforce _____ (minimum housing code, nuisance code).
- Adjust extraterritorial jurisdiction and annexation policies to _____.
- Establish design guidelines and/or historic district protections for _____.

Align the Town Government Organization

- Organize _____ (departments and staff) to align with _____ priority.
- Prioritize _____ in staff work plans.
- Train town staff for _____.
- Establish a new town position to support _____.
- Streamline _____ processes for _____.

Focus Town Finances

- Incorporate plan goals into the annual budget process to emphasize _____.
- Align the capital improvement plan with the comprehensive plan to prioritize _____.
- Adopt an urban-services boundary to _____.
- Seek public and grant funds from _____ to implement priority investments in _____.
- Evaluate public finance options for _____.
- Evaluate public property for _____.

Enhance Community Resources

- Seek designation as and follow guidelines for the North Carolina Main Street program.
- Support and maintain _____ (existing businesses, community assets, current investments).
- Identify and promote opportunity sites for _____.
- Recruit _____ businesses.
- Develop interpretive displays to highlight _____.
- Encourage property owners to protect historic structures.
- Identify and complete community beautification projects in _____.
- Identify, seek, and leverage _____ funds for _____.

Build Partnerships

- Coordinate with neighboring jurisdictions to _____.
- Partner with _____ nonprofits to _____.
- Request _____ from _____.
- Partner with _____ to coordinate regional _____.

Public Outreach and Education

- Educate the public about _____.
- Provide web-based resources to inform the public about _____.
- Establish a media campaign to raise awareness of _____.
- Coordinate outreach to _____ (specific group) to inform them about _____.
- Seek input from _____ (specific group) to learn more about _____.

Additional Research and Planning

- Initiate a small-area plan for _____ (downtown, historic district, entry corridor).
- Initiate a functional plan for _____ (pedestrian improvements, parks and recreation, bicycle facilities).
- Perform a market study for _____.
- Compile current data on _____.
- Research peer-jurisdiction approaches to _____.

Template 5B. Sample Implementation Checklist

No.	Name	Description	Priority	Staffing lead	Est. cost	Funding sources	Next steps
Short-term (1–2 years)							
Ex. 1	Development ordinance update	Revise zoning districts to match updated comprehensive plan	High	Planning dept.	$25K	General fund	Hire planning consultant
Ex. 2	Historic walking trail	Construct trail that tells story of community's founding	Medium	Planning dept., Public works	$150K	NCDOT; general fund	Hire engineering consultant to prepare plans
Medium-term (3–5 years)							
Ex. 3	Downtown park	Build park & central gathering place with events stage	High	Parks & rec., public works	$1M	Parks & rec. trust fund; general fund	Write PARTF grant proposal
Ex. 4	Main street streetscape design	Prepare design for streetscape improvements along main street	Medium	Planning dept., Public works	$50K	General fund	Hire landscape architecture consultant to prepare plans
Long-term (6–10 years)							
Ex. 5	Northeast sewer extension	Extend sewer service to northeast commercial center	Medium	Public works	$5M	USDA grant; developer fees	Conduct engineering study
Ex. 6	Community center	Construct community center	Low	Parks & rec., public works	$6M	Bond issue; general fund	Hold bond referendum

Template 6A. Plan Outline

Comprehensive and land use plans can follow many different formats and organizing schemes. This template offers one option for a plan outline that aligns with the substantive topics and process outlined in this guidebook. Note that the suggested plan summary would serve as an executive summary, giving decision makers and community members a clear overview of the process and engagement, key goals, future land use map, and priority implementation actions. Then, the outline walks through sections on each substantive topic. Appendices may be added to gather data, community input, and other key information.

Plan Summary

Summary of Process and Community Engagement
Goals / Guiding Principles
Future Land Use Map
Overview of Implementation Strategy

Natural Resources and Hazards

Current Conditions
Vision and Goals
Implementation Strategy

Community Resources and Assets

Current Conditions
Vision and Goals
Implementation Strategy

Community Development and Housing

Current Conditions
Vision and Goals
Implementation Strategy

Economic Development

Current Conditions
Vision and Goals
Implementation Strategy

Public Facilities and Infrastructure

Current Conditions
Vision and Goals
Implementation Strategy

Future Development Patterns

Appendices

Additional Detail on Process and Community Engagement Strategy
Additional Detail on Context and Current Conditions

Template 6B. Public Hearing Cheat Sheet

Once a comprehensive plan or land use plan has been drafted, there remain several steps in the process of finalizing and adopting that plan. Some of these processes are set by statute and some by ordinance. Filling out the sheet below should help you keep track of the scheduling for the plan approval process.

Please note that your zoning, land use, or unified development ordinance may include additional procedural requirements. It is recommended that you review your ordinance's rules for zoning text amendments and add whatever additional elements your ordinance might require to the table below.

Public Hearing Cheat Sheet				
Action	**Earliest date**	**Latest date**	**Reference(s)**	**Status**
Submission of proposed plan approval			n/a	
Planning board review meeting			Advice and consultation of the planning board is required by G.S. 160D-501(c). Hearing is optional; see G.S. 160D-604(a). *(Check your meeting calendar for available dates. Remember to leave plenty of time for notice!)*	
Planning board decision		30 days from referral to planning board	If no recommendation is delivered within 30 days, G.S. 160D-604(b) permits the governing board to act without input from the planning board.	
First published notice of governing board public hearing	25 days before hearing	10 days before hearing	G.S. 160D-601(a). (The notice must be published "in a newspaper having general circulation in the area.")[a]	

a. It may also be advisable to provide notice to the commander of any military base located five miles or less from the community. G.S. 160D-601(b) requires this notice if the action would change or affect permitted uses of land five miles or less from the base perimeter. It is doubtful that such a requirement would apply to a nonbinding plan, but it is possible. Notifying the base commander thus may be prudent even if it is not necessary.

Public Hearing Cheat Sheet, *continued*				
Action	**Earliest date**	**Latest date**	**Reference(s)**	**Status**
Second published notice of governing board public hearing	The calendar week after first notice	The calendar week after first notice	G.S. 160D-601(a)	
Governing board public hearing date			*(Check your meeting calendar for available dates. Also check your ordinance for any additional deadlines or time limits. Remember to leave plenty of time for notice!)*	
Governing board decision date			*(This may or may not be the same as the public hearing date.)*	

Template 7A. Sample Project Charter

This form is designed to be completed at the outset of each plan implementation project by the project sponsor, such as the town manager, and the project manager, such as the planning director.

Project Charter (insert name of project): _____				
Project purpose:				
Project sponsor:		Project manager:		
Project:		Funding source(s):		
Start date:		Completion date:		
Scope:				
Key deliverables:	1.		4.	
	2.		5.	
	3.		6.	
Key milestones:	1.		Date:	
	2.		Date:	
	3.		Date:	
	4.		Date:	
Key assumptions:	1.		3.	
	2.		4.	
Key risks/issues:	1.		3.	
	2.		4.	
Team:	1.		4.	
	2.		5.	
	3.		6.	
Partners:	1.		3.	
	2.		4.	
Success indicators:	1.		3.	
	2.		4.	